The American Welfare State

Through a practical introduction to the policies of the American welfare state—a wide-ranging subject much discussed but seldom described—this slim volume details the four main areas of social welfare policy: income assistance, housing assistance, nutrition assistance, and medical assistance. In plain, approachable language, author Brian J. Glenn explains, for example, how Section 8 housing vouchers function, what WIC is, the Medicare program, and what Temporary Aid to Needy Families does. It is written in a manner that allows a complete novice to understand these programs in a brisk and comprehensive fashion that is both short enough to assign over a couple of nights in a course and yet detailed enough for the programs to be understood at a quite nuanced level.

Due to federalism, many of these programs differ, sometimes dramatically, from locality to locality, and thus in order to understand how these programs function, Glenn looks at the support a poor household would receive in five cities: Boston, Houston, Kansas City, Los Angeles, and New Orleans. This covers not only a geographic spread, but also the range of programs from those on the higher end of the spectrum to those at the lowest levels of support, giving the reader a feel for the range of funding levels and also the variety of different ways programs can be implemented.

In short, this book is a handy teaching and research tool that a professor can assign over a night or two to fill a huge gap in the literature on a subject that many want to teach but lack the knowledge and resources to do.

Brian J. Glenn has a PhD in political science from Oxford University, has worked as a health policy analyst, and has taught at Wesleyan University, Emerson College, Hamilton College, and University of Pennsylvania. He is co-editor of *Conservatism and American Political Development*.

The American Welfare State

A Practical Guide

Brian J. Glenn

Routledge
Taylor & Francis Group
OCO857370310
NEW YORK AND LONDON

First published 2014
by Routledge
711 Third Avenue, New York, NY 10017

and by Routledge
2 Park Square, Milton Park, Abingdon, Oxon OX14 4RN

Routledge is an imprint of the Taylor & Francis Group, an informa business

© 2014 Taylor & Francis

Library of Congress Cataloging-in-Publication Data
Glenn, Brian J., 1969–
   The American welfare state : a practical guide / Brian J. Glenn.
      pages cm
   1. Public welfare—United States.   2. Welfare state—United States.
3. United States—Social policy.   I. Title.
   HV95.G536 2013
   361.6'50973—dc23
   2013034765

ISBN: 978-0-415-73004-4 (hbk)
ISBN: 978-0-415-73005-1 (pbk)
ISBN: 978-1-315-85062-7 (ebk)

Typeset in ApexBembo
by Apex CoVantage, LLC

Printed and bound in the United States of America by Publishers Graphics, LLC on sustainably sourced paper.

To all those who formed my safety net over the years, especially Tom Baker, now at the University of Pennsylvania School of Law, and Marc Landy, of Boston College.

Contents

List of Illustrations

Tables

Preface

This book stemmed from a course entitled "The Development of the American Welfare State" I taught first at Emerson College and then at Wesleyan University. I wanted my students to understand what policy analysts meant when we talked about "the American welfare state." Alas, I simply could not find a useful source, so I did the most obvious thing one does in situations like that: I wrote a book.

It has been very hard being objective in my discussions of the policies presented below, and I have worked very hard to keep my own political beliefs as distant as possible so that this book can be seen as a useful tool for people across the political spectrum. Even still, I was surprised at how often I was struck at some deep level in researching the social safety net woven by the various localities. How we treat ourselves and others in times of need speaks very deeply to how we understand ourselves as a polity, and if nothing else, it is fascinating to see how differently the five states discussed below can treat the same needy individuals and families.

You will also see that I cite almost no academic literature on this vast range of topics. Rest assured, it is not because I haven't read it. Rather it is because I wanted this book to focus on one topic and one topic only, and that is the programs the federal government, state governments, and localities create to support those who lack the financial means to support themselves.

The exciting part of creating a book like this is that social safety net programs are constantly changing, and watching policy innovations is fascinating. We simultaneously think about the ethical implications of how those in need are treated, and also whether the programs will achieve their goals—if it is even clear what the goals are. Then we start to think about how we would measure success, which is of course what makes policy analysis so intellectually stimulating.

Of course, the fact that policies are constantly evolving also means that there will be elements discussed below that will sooner or later be out-of-date, and while on the one hand I wish everything in this book were constantly up-to-date, on the other, the goal is to get you to the point where you understand these programs well enough to research them on your own.

On that note, while I was writing first a small version and then the larger version that ended up becoming this book, I also assigned the research found below to my students and Emerson and Wesleyan, and I wish I had been able to tell them at the time how much it meant to me that while I was the professor and they were the students, we were also colleagues. Watching my students struggle to understand the programs I had managed to get my hands around not that long prior brought me much closer to them, and even after several years have passed, many of them continue to email me with articles they have read. With that being said, if you find that policies have evolved, please do contact me with the updated information, so that I can pass that on to others. The world of policy analysis is both big and small. Big in that there are many of us. Small in that it is remarkably easy to reach out to others.

Acknowledgments

The unsung heroes behind any policy analyst are the research librarians who help us track down those facts and figures that we are know are there but which are initially hidden. Nicole Brown, then of Emerson College, and Erhard Konerding of Wesleyan University were fantastic. My "Development of the American Welfare State" students at Emerson and Wesleyan served as wonderful springboards, enthusiastically heading out into the internet, local assistance offices, and in one case, asking a parent who happened to be a high-level administrator, to find their own data. Their enthusiasm kept me going through the challenge of taking a wide array of programs across five cities and producing something that a non-expert can comprehend. It is hard to explain how much students can touch our lives, and I am grateful to all of those who have.

Two important individuals facilitated my students' research. Peter Hess, then of Emerson College, and Kevin Wiliarty, then of Wesleyan University, were the academic support ITS professionals who helped me set up some incredible websites and blogs for my students. Research is a collaborative effort, and Peter and Kevin made my students' research much easier through the use of technology. While I conducted my research prior to assigning it to my students, I cannot deny that having scores of really intelligent folks verify what I had found was greatly appreciated, and I would be dishonest if I failed to acknowledge they uncovered a policy or two that I had not spotted.

Finally, I want to thank all the social workers and research staff in various government departments who helped me track down numbers that were not publicly available, or make sense of how certain elements were implemented. As I mention at several points in this book, social workers keep the system running, for many of the programs discussed below are extremely hard to understand, even for a professional policy analyst, and for those in need of the assistance the programs provide, social workers form the gateway to getting the needy into them. Until I began researching this book, I had no idea just how important they are, and my respect for what they do is now immense.

List of Abbreviations

ADC	Aid to Dependent Children
AFDC	Aid to Families with Dependent Children
AHVP	Alternative Housing Voucher Program
ALS	Amyotrophic Lateral Sclerosis
AMI	Area's Median Income
APTC	Advanced Premium Tax Credit
BHA	Boston Housing Authority
CACFP	Child and Adult Care Food Program
CAP	Combined Application Process
CAPI	Cash Assistance Program for Immigrants
CARE	California Alternative Rates for Energy
CCAP	Child Care Assistance Program (Louisiana)
CCR&R	Child Care Resource and Referral
CHIP	Children's Health Insurance Program
CMSP	Children's Medical Security Plan
COBRA	Combined Omnibus Budget Reconciliation Act
CSFP	Commodity Supplemental Food Program
CTTP	California Tribal TANF Program
DPA	Down Payment Assistance
DSS	Department of Social Services
DTA	Department of Transitional Assistance
EAEDC	Emergency Aid to Elders, Disabled and Children
EBT	Electronic Benefit Transfer (card)
EITC	Earned Income Tax Credit
FDPIR	Food Distribution Program on Indian Reservations
FFVP	Fresh Fruit and Vegetable Program
FITAP	Family Independence Temporary Assistance Program
FNS	Food and Nutrition Service (USDA)
FPHP	Fishing Partnership Health Plan
FPL	Federal Poverty Line or Federal Poverty Limit
FSET	Food Stamp Employment and Training (program)
FSS	Family Self-Sufficiency Program

FS/WP	Food Stamp Work Program
GR	General Relief
GROW	General Relief Opportunities for Work
HACLA	Housing Authority of the City of Los Angeles
HACoLA	Housing Authority of the County of Los Angeles
HANO	Housing Authority of New Orleans
HAP	Housing Assistance Program of Greater Kansas City
HCTC	Health Coverage Tax Credit
HCVP	Housing Choice Voucher Program
H-EAT	Heat and Eat Program
HHA	Houston Housing Authority
HMO	Health Maintenance Organization (plan)
HOP	Home Ownership Program
HOPWA	Housing Opportunities for People with AIDS
HPRP	Homeless Prevention and Rapid Re-Housing Program
HUD	Department of Housing and Urban Development
HUD-VASH	Housing and Urban Development Veteran Affairs Supportive Housing
KCSP	Kinship Care Subsidy Program (Louisiana)
LaCAP	Louisiana Combined Application Process
LACDC	Los Angeles Community Development Commission
LA GAIN	Los Angeles Greater Avenues for Independence
LIHEAP	Low Income Heating Energy Assistance Program
LSHSCP	Louisiana State Head Start Collaboration Project
MAGI	Modified Annual Gross Income
MBR	Medical Benefits Request
MRVP	Massachusetts Rental Voucher Program
MSP	Medical Security Plan
NSBP	National School Breakfast (program)
NSLP	National School Lunch (program)
PCC	Primary Care Clinician (plan)
PHA	Public Housing Authority
PPACA	Patient Protection and Affordable Care Act
PRWORA	Personal Responsibility and Work Opportunity Reconciliation Act of 1996
SNAP	Supplemental Nutrition Assistance Program
SRO	Single Room Occupancy Program
SSDI	Social Security Disability Insurance
SSI	Supplemental Security Income
SSP	State Supplemental Program
STEP	Strategies to Empower People
SUA	Standard Utility Allowance
TA	Temporary Aid
TAA	Trade Adjustment Assistance

TAFDC	Temporary Aid to Families with Dependent Children
TANF	Temporary Aid to Needy Families
TEFAP	The Emergency Food Assistance Program
TEXT MSG	Teaching Empowerment to Exit Transitional Housing by Managing Secure Goals
TRA	Trade Adjustment Allowance
TWC	Texas Workforce Commission
UI	Unemployment Insurance
USDA	Department of Agriculture
WC	Worker's Compensation
WIC	Special Supplemental Program for Women, Infants and Children
WTW	Welfare to Work
VA	Department of Veterans Affairs

Chapter 1

Some Introductory Thoughts on the American Welfare State

The "American welfare state" is a subject often discussed but rarely described. Our images of it are all too often shaped by individuals promoting one political cause or another, leaving us with a distorted understanding of this important topic. Indeed, the biggest challenge anyone faces in discussing the social safety net created to support the nation's poor is the very political nature of the subject. It is extremely difficult to talk about anti-poverty programs objectively, because these policies speak to the very core of the understanding of who we are as a nation. In this book, I try very hard to paint as objective a picture as possible, since I hope this little volume will be seen as a useful resource by people across the political spectrum.

The American Welfare State is divided by chapter into the four traditional categories of housing, nutrition, income, and medical assistance, as they exist in five geographically distributed cities, as those programs existed in the middle of 2013. The cities are: Boston, Massachusetts; Houston, Texas; Kansas City, Kansas (and sometimes also Missouri); Los Angeles, California; and New Orleans, Louisiana. As we shall see, these five cites, some smaller, some huge, some endowed with tremendous financial capacity, others less so, offer a wide range of programs, some of which are innovative and thoughtful, while others may feel outdated. Some programs are closed to new participants or have waitlists that can extend for years, while others literally begin operating the moment an applicant applies. While keeping the descriptions brief, the goal of the book is to show the reader what governmentally provided programs are available to poor households in America—what we call "the welfare state."[1] Clearly there are programs that fall outside of the categories the book employs, such as after-school literacy programs and many efforts to feed and clothe the needy through charity, for example, and to cover all of these would require volumes.

That being said, there are certain charities that are not directly connected to the government but that are so central to the story that they simply must be mentioned, if only to allow researchers a good starting point for exploration beyond what is covered here. For the most part, however, not-for-profits will only be mentioned if they are directly part of the welfare state, by which we mean the system of assistance created by the three levels of government to support the nation's neediest citizens. As we shall see, much assistance for the needy is *funded* by the government, but *provided* privately, such as through vouchers that allow families to rent on the private market, programs that help low-income employees pay for health insurance provided through their employers, or the Boys and Girls Clubs of America, which are reimbursed by the government to provide free lunches to impoverished children when school is not in session.

Beyond presenting the programs, a key aim of this book is to make them easily understandable. For each of the four categories of housing, nutrition, income and medical assistance, the various programs and benefits available to poor households will be described, as clearly and parsimoniously as possible, in the text. The goal is to cover all the major programs and all of their major subcategories. The book frequently goes into greater detail about specific programs in the tables, allowing for a deeper understanding of eligibility requirements for example, or the types of benefits available. Thus, those who are merely looking for an overview of the American welfare state can simply read the text while skipping the data in the tables. Those seeking more detail will find it there, along with ample citations so you can go straight to the source.

Almost all of the programs, with the few exceptions of a couple that are targeted at the elderly or military veterans, are means tested, which is to say that to be eligible, an individual or household must fall below a certain income and/or asset level. The guideline used is almost always in relationship to the Federal Poverty Line (also called the Federal Poverty Level or Federal Poverty Guideline). Some programs target those directly at or below the Federal Poverty Line (FPL), while other programs will target those who fall a certain percentage above or below it. The 2013 Federal Poverty Line levels are found in Table 1.1. As can be seen from the second column, the

Table 1.1 2013 Federal Poverty Line by Household Size, for the District of Columbia and all States (except Alaska and Hawaii)[2]

Size of family unit	100 Percent of Poverty	133 Percent of Poverty	150 Percent of Poverty	200 Percent of Poverty	400 Percent of Poverty
1	$11,490	$15,282	$17,235	$22,980	$ 45,960
2	$15,510	$20,628	$23,265	$31,020	$ 62,040
3	$19,530	$25,975	$29,295	$39,060	$ 78,120
4	$23,550	$31,322	$35,325	$47,100	$ 94,200
5	$27,570	$36,668	$41,355	$55,140	$110,280
6	$31,590	$42,015	$47,385	$63,180	$126,360
7	$35,610	$47,361	$53,415	$71,220	$142,440
8	$39,630	$52,708	$59,445	$79,260	$158,520

poverty line is $11,490 for an individual, $15,510 for a household of two, and $19,530 for a household of three.

The Federal Poverty Line was created over 1963 and 1964 by a Social Security Administration researcher named Mollie Orshansky. The Department of Agriculture had developed four food plans that were assumed to be adequate for households of different sizes, and Orshansky developed her thresholds based on the economy food plan (now called the thrifty Food Plan), which was the cheapest of the four. From the 1955 Census she figured that a household spent roughly one-third of its budget on food, and thus started with the economy plan and then multiplied it by three.[3] That methodology has been continued to the present day. "Phantom shoppers" are routinely sent to grocery stores across the nation with a shopping list, which they price out. This data is then compiled and used to set the FPL, which is set once a year and is applicable for the next twelve months.

In October 2013, the health insurance marketplaces created by the Affordable Care Act began taking applications, using a different measure. Eligibility for assistance in the marketplaces look not at gross income, but rather Modified Annual Gross Income (MAGI), which factors in both more expenses and more income sources than plain old gross income does, allowing for a more accurate depiction of a household's income. It is quite possible that over the next few years, many of the programs discussed below will convert to employing MAGI for their income testing, since it is both a more accurate reflection of income, and also will make aligning programs with the health insurance marketplaces easier.[4]

On that note, it is important to say at the start that the programs discussed in this book are constantly evolving. On the one hand, this means that we constantly need to verify that information is accurate, although income and asset limits typically are only readjusted once a year, allowing recipients and those who implement the programs some stability. It is quite rare to see a new program emerge, and even rarer to see one disbanded, but internally, programs evolve—especially after elections where one party takes over from another. While this is daunting for the researcher, since we must always fear that we missed something, it is also rather exciting. States really do serve as "laboratories of democracy," to use Justice Brandeis's phrase,[5] allowing us to study what works and what does not, or more accurately, what seems to work better and what seems to be less effective, hopefully, over time, leading to programs that are better able to achieve their stated goals.

At the time of publication, this book is standing at the very cutting edge of perhaps the most important policy development since the Great Society programs emerged in the 1960s. This, of course, is the implementation of the Affordable Care Act, which will be discussed in detail in the healthcare chapter. It is extremely rare to see changes of such scope emerge in a policy realm, and putting aside judgments about whether or not one agrees with it politically, from the perspective of a policy analyst, this is as exciting as it gets. On a state-by-state basis, the nation is redefining its social safety net, and doing so in a profoundly American manner. As of January 1, 2014, every legal resident of the nation is required either to have health insurance, or pay a tax that will get larger for each of the following years. But the government itself will not provide insurance; private companies will continue to do so. Once again, we see the public/private mix that will appear over and over in the chapters that follow. Moreover, the states have a variety of ways to implement the ACA, and even inside of the three main categories of implementation, the variation will still be enormous.

Hopefully this book will help you get your hands around the welfare state enough to understand what is available to poor households in the five locations under examination. The larger goal is to empower you to study the location of your own choosing and make sense of what you find there. To that end, this book is less about providing answers than helping conceptualize the questions you might want to ask, along with arming you to answer them on your own.

The American Welfare State

Outsiders will often smirk at the concept of an American welfare state. "There isn't one" is a common refrain. Of course there is one, but it is a patchwork, provided by at least three different levels of government (cities, states, and the federal government), whose leaders may be driven by very different electoral incentives, while even within one level, programs are often not very well coordinated. Federal programs are created by Congress, which is itself divided into committees whose members, again, may face very different electoral incentives from members of other committees, and there simply is not enough reason for them to coordinate anti-poverty programs. Indeed, many members support their programs not because they are anti-poverty programs at all, but rather because those programs assist other constituents. The most obvious example is that of nutrition programs, overseen by the House and Senate Agriculture Committees. While as policy researchers, we look at these programs for their effects of feeding the needy, many members of the Agriculture Committees may look at the same programs as ways to support their farmers back home. Other programs are overseen by congressional Labor Committees, and even others by Health and Human Services or Education. Thus, part of the reason for the patchwork nature of federal programs is simply that the body tasked with creating and funding them is not organized in a way that allows it to take a holistic approach to the matter.

There is also the issue of federalism, or the division of political power between different levels of government. The challenge that county or municipal governments face is that if they tax too high or provide benefits that are more supportive than their neighbors, the wealthier residents may move out and the poorer may move in. The empirical evidence for this actually happening is actually quite thin, largely because the poor are quite immobile. Poor people rely on mutual assistance networks of friends and family for support in ways that tie them to their local communities. I watch your kids on Mondays, you watch mine on Tuesdays, someone fixes cars when they break down, another does people's hair. Many poor people survive on remarkably small amounts of income because they have woven themselves into barter communities that allow them to receive and provide services without money ever changing hands. To move elsewhere, even for a much better job, may still not benefit them if they have to start paying for all those previously bartered services. While at the other end, those with means may not like paying higher taxes, but will still choose to live where they desire for no other reason that they can afford to do so. Nonetheless, state and local officials feel great pressure to keep spending on social services low, and to keep their taxes low as well. When they do feel pressured to spend, it is often on areas that promote local industry, such as infrastructure like roads and bridges, and if the poor benefit from these incentives at all, it is typically through receiving training to meet the needs of local businesses.[6]

In addition to the institutional factors just discussed, the welfare state also has a cultural inheritance, of which there are two elements. First, the cultures that dominated American society in the colonial era bequeathed an understanding of deservingness that was attached to work, and this has been handed down across the centuries, up to the present day. The second element has to do with race.

It is difficult to tell a cultural story in any meaningful way in just a page or two, but in short, the original colonies were dominated by three cultures—each of which was far from monolithic but still generally held the same beliefs about poverty. In the north, the majority of Americans subscribed to the Puritan doctrine of predestination, which is the belief that God had a plan for each individual and that the goal in life was to live according to His will. A central element of doing so entailed engaging in hard work. The Puritans took care of the needy in their local communities, often with great concern and kindness, but this extended only to those who could not help themselves.

The town would take in elderly widows, who would spend two weeks in each family's house, for example, while those who were injured in an accident might have their farms looked after. Still, most of the focus of towns was on taking care of orphans, who were usually apprenticed until they reached adult age. Those who were not able to care for themselves were more often than not treated very humanely. But for people who were considered lazy ("idle" was the term of the times) the story was quite different. "For those who indulge themselves in idleness, the express command of

God unto us is, that we should let them starve," wrote Rev. Cotton Mather.[7] Poor outsiders who wanted to move into towns were sometimes driven to the border, while residents who did not appear to want to work could be whipped or have their children taken from them. What is so interesting is that for the Puritans, hard work did not lead to wealth, since they believed in predestination. In other words, God willed that some would be wealthy and others poor, and one's place in life was not connected to how hard one worked. Rather, one worked to please God, who still might choose to keep one poor. In any event, the result of this form of thinking was that everyone should work, and those who could not would be protected while those who could but did not were left to get by on their own.

The Southern Protestants did not believe in predestination, but adopted pretty much the same thinking about the nature of poverty. While often not as wealthy as their northern counterparts, southern localities also taxed themselves to care for the poor and needy amongst them. Often the poor were cared for by the local church leaders, who were tasked with distributing the community's funds.

Even after Puritanism faded as a religion and the dominant belief of New England, the system of thought about the "deserving" who could not help themselves and the able-bodied "undeserving" remained in the social safety nets that the following generations wove. Up and down the expanding nation's eastern seaboard and deep into the Midwest, keeping people in their own homes or the homes of their neighbors came to be replaced in the 1800s with institutional forms of care: boarding schools for handicapped children coupled with orphanages for children without parents who could care for them. Massive "mental asylums" were built for those with psychiatric problems, along with reform schools for children who had problems with the law. While localities continued to provide some families (usually those headed by widows) with small donations of cash to pay rent, or in-kind services such as firewood or coal, the rest of the needy were forced to rely on poorhouses. Poorhouses provided room and board, but were also meant to have a reform function for the able-bodied, since they were informed by the belief that those who were able to work should always be able to find employment, and those who did not had a problem with their work ethic.

By all accounts, poorhouses were simply terrible places, and they were so by design since taxpayers resented having to fund them, and again, they were intended to be so awful that the able-bodied would want to avoid them. When researchers conducted censuses of poorhouse residents, the data showed something very different. Poorhouses had very few able-bodied men in them and were populated by large numbers of elderly who lacked children nearby who could care for them. They also had large numbers of widows or abandoned wives, and many of these women had children in orphanages. Policymakers and the staff of these institutions began to ask why the taxpayer were paying for women to stay in awful poorhouses and their children in equally dreadful orphanages when, for roughly similar amounts of funding, these women and children could stay together in their own homes. Similar arguments were made about the elderly.

Thus, at the dawn of the twenty-first century, Americans confronted the time-old question of how to care for the "deserving" while keeping the "undeserving" from the rolls? Underpinning all of this was the question of race. It is extremely hard to find any evidence of black people receiving assistance from a local government, and where they had the resources, they set up their own mutual assistance societies and banks, but these were usually quite lacking in adequate funds, since the legal system was so heavily stacked against them. The "deserving" always referred only to white people, both in the north and the south, and looking at discussions of the elderly, impoverished women, and the care of children, one often finds frank references to "preserving the white race" and also of Protestantism (since Catholics were the wrong kind of white). As localities slowly pulled the elderly, mothers, and children out of institutions and began giving them funds to pay for food and rent instead, local charity boards and relief organizations carefully scrutinized applicants to ensure they fell on the "right" side of the social cleavage.

The Social Security Act of 1935 embodied a profound shift in the relationship between the citizens and the state, but was still informed by the two themes of work and race. The Act was massive, with many elements, but for our purposes, we can focus on just three, old-age insurance, Aid to Dependent Children (ADC), and Supplemental Security Income (SSI). Although it was initially considered the least important element (since it was not supposed to go into effect immediately), the element we typically refer to today as "Social Security" is the retirement element, officially known as the Old-Age, Survivors, and Disability Insurance program. Under the retirement element of the Act, workers and their employers pay a certain percentage of their income from each paycheck into the system; this is the "FICA" line on your paycheck. As long as someone has worked at least twenty quarters over their lifetime, they are eligible for a monthly payment once they retire, which is pegged to inflation. For our purposes, it may be useful to conceptualize the old-age retirement element as *anti-poverty insurance,* given that this has, in fact, done a remarkably good job at lifting seniors on it out of poverty.

The retirement element was influenced by race, however. The original Act exempted two groups from coverage: self-employed farmers and domestic help. These two professions, of course, were precisely where very large percentages of black Americans worked, and was the price that southern senators and congressmen exacted from President Roosevelt for their support. These exemptions ended under President Eisenhower, who saw the expansion of Social Security as his greatest domestic policy achievement.

Finally, there was Aid to Dependent Children, the precursor to today's Temporary Aid to Needy Families. This program, too, was racially structured. Partially funded by the federal government, partially by the states, this program provided cash assistance to poor children and their parents, but the qualifications for how much support and who received it were left to the states. Most states, northern and southern, required parents to be of "good character," which unfortunately was used as code to ensure that very few non-white recipients found their way onto the rolls until such discrimination was banned in the 1960s.

The one notable element that did not find its way into the Social Security Act of 1935 was health insurance. Unions and many mutual benefit societies opposed it because it was a benefit they offered to their members, and they feared they would be weakened if one of their primary benefits was undercut. Large employers also offered it to their most valued skilled employees and saw it as a way to attract and retain key workers. Physicians were worried about government intervention in their finances. As a result, health insurance eventually became a benefit offered by employers to their workers, a legacy that remains to this very day despite many attempts to make it a federal benefit over the ensuing decades.

But what of those who did not work? Those households paid out-of-pocket for their medical expenses, and when Lyndon Baines Johnson rose to the presidency, he added two major elements to the American social safety net. The first was Medicare, which offered medical insurance to the retired. Those who were eligible for Social Security, that is, those who had worked and paid taxes during their younger years now qualify for Medicare when they turn sixty-five. Medicare has different components to it, but in essence, all on it have the option of receiving coverage for preventative medicine, inpatient and outpatient care, and costs for medication.

The second program created by Johnson's "Great Society" is Medicaid, the medical program for the poor. This program is *means tested,* so that to qualify for it, one must fall below certain income and asset limits. These will be discussed in detail below. Medicaid also offers comprehensive medical coverage, but does not pay hospitals and physicians as much as either Medicare or commercial health insurance plans do, and sometimes recipients have difficulty finding a provider who will service them.

One final element needs to be mentioned. In 1939, Social Security was altered to provide benefits to the dependent spouses and children of deceased workers, until those children reached adulthood. Unlike ADC (or Aid to Families with Dependent Children, AFDC, as the program came to be named before once again getting renamed Temporary Aid to Needy Families in 1996) which never lifted families out of poverty, Social Security's benefits could do so. Meaning that if the family's main breadwinner had been earning above-poverty wages and had been working, most likely the dependants would remain above poverty, while those who turned to AFDC/ TANF did not. This had a profound racial impact on the nature of the recipients in each program. Due to the higher likelihood that white mothers were both married and married to employed men who had earned above-poverty wages, an extremely high percentage of white widows and children who lost the husbands went into the Social Security system, while the exact opposite happened to black women and children, who went into AFDC. Social Security, pegged to earnings, has remained incredibly popular throughout the decades, while AFDC/TANF, what many typically refer to as "welfare," has been under literally constant attack as too generous and expensive, almost from the start.

As an inheritance of what has gone before, we now have a system in America that is structured by work. If someone works full-time and receives benefits, they can get their health insurance through their employer, along with other benefits such as sick time, vacations, and retirement plans. If the main breadwinner passes away early, the spouse and underage dependent children will receive benefits from Social Security that quite likely will keep them above the poverty line. Workers and spouses who live to be sixty-five will get their health insurance through Medicare, and a retirement pension from Social Security. Those who are not working, or who are not working in a job that pays them a wage that lifts them above poverty, will instead have to turn to Temporary Aid to Needy Families for assistance. This program will not give them benefits that lift them above the poverty line. They will get their health insurance through Medicaid, if they fall before a certain income limit, or through the new health insurance marketplaces, purchasing plans that are subsidized through federal tax credits plus whatever assistance the given state they reside in chooses to offer. If they do not contribute through working to Social Security while they are young, they will not receive benefits when they are older, nor will they be able to go onto Medicare.

Thus we find ourselves with the social safety system we have, mostly funded by the federal government, with additional (often grudging or contractually forced through cost-sharing) assistance from the states, with localities offering a wide range of programs as well. As we shall see, public–private partnerships abound, from housing and homeless shelters, to training programs and daycare centers, to soup kitchens and programs that feed children when schools aren't in session, to community health centers. Finally, we will see very clear divisions between programs that are means tested and those received by right of simply having worked and paid taxes.

Notes

1 Even the term "household" is tricky. In a work like this, one must always go to the source, but just so we can move forward, we will use the definition employed by the federal Department of Housing and Urban Development. HUD allows a "group of persons" to be connected by blood, marriage or operation of law, or the group must provide evidence of a significant relationship determined to be stable by the housing authority. http://www3.lacdc.org/CDCWebsite/AH/linkit.aspx?id=476 (accessed August 2013).

2   78 FR 5182, January 24, 2013 (https://www.federalregister.gov/articles/2013/01/24/2013-01422/annual-update-of-the-hhs-poverty-guidelines). Table also compiled with data from http://www.familiesusa.org/resources/tools-for-advocates/guides/federal-poverty-guidelines.html (accessed August 2013).

3   http://aspe.hhs.gov/poverty/papers/hptgssiv.htm (accessed August 2013).

4   A point we will discuss later is that most people involved with social programs, it is safe to say, would love to see the same set of criteria be used for programs across the board, which would not only make their job of getting needy individuals into the programs for which they are eligible easier, but would also allow for "one-stop shopping" where an applicant who is eligible for one program is automatically enrolled in all the others as well.

5   285 U.S. 262.

6   Paul E. Peterson. *City Limits*. Chicago: University of Chicago Press, 1981.

7   Walter I. Trattner. 1999. *From Poor Law to Welfare State: A History of Social Welfare in America*. New York: Free Press, 23.

Chapter 2

Income Assistance

The first category of American welfare state programs we will examine seeks to help recipients primarily through providing them with financial resources that can be used at the recipient's discretion, as opposed, for example, to what many still call "food stamps," which can only be used for very specific purchases. Two programs, Unemployment Insurance and Worker's Compensation, seek to replace a portion of a worker's wages during periods when they either cannot find a job or cannot work due to getting injured on the job, respectively. These two programs are not means tested and instead are pegged to the individual's previous income and thus can provide recipients with above-poverty levels of support, although for limited periods of time. With the exception of Social Security survivor's benefits, the other programs discussed in this chapter provide recipients with levels of support that will not lift them out of poverty in order to encourage recipients to find gainful employment.

The largest income support program by far is Temporary Aid to Needy Families (TANF), which will be discussed in more detail below. As we shall see, many of the programs discussed in this section do much more than simply replace income that otherwise would have been earned through work (otherwise referred to as "earned income"). Indeed, TANF is perhaps best understood as a basket of goods, the most valuable, to be certain, being income support, but there are also many other elements to it.

Unemployment Insurance[1]

Unemployment Insurance (UI) is partially funded through the federal Department of Labor (under the Federal Unemployment Tax Act) and is administered by the respective states, which often employ very different models for funding the programs, although from the perspective of the recipients, they are largely the same. Workers who have lost their jobs through no fault of their own are eligible for up to twenty-six weeks of benefits, although there have been extensions due to the severe recession the nation has been experiencing since 2008. "No fault of one's own," of course, needs to be defined. Looking to Texas, it means either being laid off or having one's hours reduced, having to quit for medical reasons or to protect one's family, or to accommodate a military spouse (there is a penalty if the spouse is non-military).[2]

UI benefits are tied to one's earnings, and the percentage of income being replaced varies from state to state. In Texas, earnings are calculated by averaging income according to a formula best described by the Texas Workforce Commission:

> To receive benefits you must have a payable claim. A payable claim means you earned a specific amount of wages during a recent 12-month period called the base period. The base period is the first four of the last five completed calendar quarters before you applied for benefits. (Calendar quarters are three-month periods beginning the first day of January, April, July, or October.) This means that when we calculate benefits we cannot use wages in the calendar quarter in which you filed your claim, or the quarter just before that. We calculate your *weekly benefit amount* on the highest quarter earnings in your base period. We divide that high quarter's total earnings by 25 to get your weekly benefit amount. We may have to adjust this amount to be inside the allowed range of benefit amounts in Texas. Your weekly benefit amount will be between $61 and $426 depending upon the wages you earned. Your maximum or total benefit amount is the lesser of 26 times the weekly amount, or 27 percent of all your wages in the base period.[3]

In plain English, Texas will calculate an average wage for the four quarters an individual worked (prior to the last two), and then provide roughly one-quarter of those wages, but not less than $61 a week or more than $426.[4]

Recipients in California, on the other hand, may receive up to half of their previous wages, up to a limit of not more than $450 per week.[5] Recipients can still work part-time and receive benefits, but will see their UI benefits cut by a certain amount. If one earns more than $25 a week but less than $100, any earnings over the first $25 will be matched by cuts to that amount, so that if one earns $50 in a week, benefits will be cut by $25. If one earns over $101 a week, the first 25 percent of income is ignored and the rest is matched by cuts.[6] Applicants must be able to work and must actively seek work, and are required to accept any full-time position they are offered. Working full-time at any job at any wage renders one ineligible for staying on Unemployment Insurance.

To be eligible for UI in Texas, one needs to have been employed in at least two of the four quarters forming the base period for wages that total at least thirty-seven times the weekly benefit amount, and the applicant must have earned at least six times the new weekly amount since the time he or she qualified for benefits on a prior claim, which in short, is meant to ensure that those applying for Unemployment Insurance were actually at some point employed and earned at least some substantial amount for their labors.[7] Second, the applicant must demonstrate that he or she is unemployed due to no fault of his or her own, the evidence of which is usually provided by the last employer. Finally, the applicant must document that they are applying for work, and register to search online at WorkInTexas.com. As mentioned above, UI recipients must actively look for work, and are obligated to accept offers that are within their previous salary range. That limit drops as time on UI goes by.[8]

Trade Adjustment Assistance

Some people lose their jobs because the position folds and is sent overseas, where the cost of labor is cheaper, and to deal with this situation, Congress created a federal program, Trade Adjustment Assistance (TAA), to protect workers harmed either by their firm going under due to cheaper imports, or because their job was moved overseas. The program was initiated under the Trade Expansion Act of 1962 and reauthorized under the Trade Act of 1974, and then again under the Trade and Globalization Adjustment Act of 2009 which expired on February 13, 2011.[9] (Note that while the program is no longer taking new applications, there may still be individuals in the program.) The TAA is divided into four sections for farmers, employees, employers, and communities, with each section being administered by the federal Departments of Agriculture, Labor, and Commerce (for the latter two) respectfully. But from the perspective of the applicant, everyone goes to just one state source.

In Texas, that is, again, the Texas Workforce Commission. In effect, participants in TAA receive many of the benefits of those enrolled in TANF (discussed below); indeed, many are designed to assist recipients once their TANF benefits expire.[10] Participants enter into WorkInTexas.com and receive the same job search assistance, help with relocation expenses if moving elsewhere, assistance for training, income support (called Trade Readjustment Allowances [TRA]—those over 50 get a supplement—once their TANF benefits expire),[11] and a Health Coverage Tax Credit (HCTC) to offset part of the costs of having to purchase healthcare on one's own.[12]

Worker's Compensation

Worker's Compensation, almost always referred to as Worker's Comp, is governed by the federal Department of Labor and administered by the respective states, although employers in Texas need not enter into the system (although, of course, the companies will still be liable).[13] Worker's Comp is designed to protect workers injured on the job by allowing them to receive healthcare and up to 60 percent of their wages while they are recovering. Table 2.1

Table 2.1 Worker's Compensation Benefits in Kansas[14]

Date of Injury	Maximum Weekly Compensation			Maximum Total Compensation					
	Weekly Benefit	Statewide Average Weekly Wage	SAWW Calendar Year	Permanent Total Disability	Temporary Total or Permanent Partial Disability	Death	Funeral Expense	Unauthorized Medical Expenses	Medical and Hospital
July 1, 2013–June 30, 2014	$587.00	$782.51	2012	$155,000	$130,000	$300,000	$5,000	$500	No limit
July 1, 2012–June 30, 2013	$570.00	$760.09	2011	$155,000	$130,000	$300,000	$5,000	$500	No limit
July 1, 2011–June 30, 2012	$555.00	$740.40	2010	$155,000	$130,000	$300,000	$5,000	$500	No limit
May 15, 2011–June 30, 2011	$545.00	$726.11	2009	$155,000	$130,000	$300,000	$5,000	$500	No limit
July 1, 2010–May 14, 2011	$545.00	$726.11	2009	$125,000	$100,000	$250,000	$5,000	$500	No limit
July 1, 2009–June 30, 2010	$546.00	$727.69	2008	$125,000	$100,000	$250,000	$5,000	$500	No limit
July 1, 2008–June 30, 2009	$529.00	$705.35	2007	$125,000	$100,000	$250,000	$5,000	$500	No limit
July 1, 2007–June 30, 2008	$510.00	$679.81	2006	$125,000	$100,000	$250,000	$5,000	$500	No limit

summarizes the benefits provided by Worker's Compensation in Kansas. An injured worker is entitled to all the medical treatments necessary to cure or relieve the effects of the injury, although the employer has the right to choose the authorizing physician. If an injured worker does not like the physician, he or she can go elsewhere, but the employer is liable only for the first $500 in expenses. The injured worker will not be compensated for the loss of the first week's wages, but after that will get two-thirds of his or her gross weekly wages, up to the maximum listed in Table 2.1. Temporary Total Disability benefits are paid when the worker is completely unable to engage in gainful employment, and are paid for the duration of the illness. If a worker loses any combination of: both eyes, both hands or arms, both feet or legs, they are automatically considered permanently injured, although they may also be considered this for sustaining other harm. If the worker is killed and has dependants, they will receive survivors' benefits, in addition to $5,000 for funeral expenses.[15]

Worker's Comp is not an anti-poverty program in theory, but rather a system set up by the various states in the early decades of the 1900s to allow workers injured on the job to receive compensation while they recovered, without having to go to court. In most states, employers pay into a form of insurance fund. The more a particular company's employees draw on the fund, the more that company has to pay in, giving employers an incentive to make their workplaces safer. In practice, though, Worker's Comp is very much an anti-poverty program, because those who draw upon it the most are people who perform physical labor for a wage, and who would be dropped into poverty very quickly if they were forced to go weeks to months without pay while they recovered.

Benefits to Disabled Veterans

States also provide benefits, large and small, to disabled veterans.[16] California provides a free parks and recreation pass.[17] Louisiana provides pensions.[18] Missouri offers property tax abatements.[19] Texas has programs for purchasing residential property and land, along with property tax abatements.[20] Massachusetts exempts disabled veterans from property taxes, the motor vehicles tax, and the state sales tax, and provides a $2,000 annuity annually.[21] All states waive tuition to their public colleges and universities, offer free fishing and hunting licenses, motor vehicle licenses (and usually registration fees), burials at state and federal veterans' cemeteries, various forms of vocational rehabilitation, and free or subsidized residence at state veterans' homes (some of these will be discussed later on in more detail). Most of these programs are not means tested and are hard to categorize as being part of the social safety net, but they all do strive to make life less expensive for those who have lost their capacity to earn because of injuries sustained while serving their country.

Earned Income Tax Credit and Earned Income Credit

When policymakers sought ways to encourage those at the very bottom of the income scale to earn more income, one method they settled upon was to apply the full tax on wages gradually, rather than all at once, allowing poorer workers to keep a higher percentage of their wages than better paid workers would. The federal government and many states, including Kansas, Missouri, Louisiana, and Massachusetts (but not California, and Texas does not have a personal income tax) have programs woven into their income tax systems, with the federal credit being called the Earned Income Tax Credit (EITC) and the one from the states sometimes referred to as an Earned Income Credit. At the state level, the formulas for calculating returns are complicated, and are much easier to qualify for if the worker has dependent children. For the 2013 tax year, single workers without children have to have earned less than $14,340 to qualify for a credit, $37,870 if they have one child, and a worker with two children less than $43,038. Married couples add $5,040 to those limits. Single individuals without dependants must be at least twenty-five years old, and finally, the tax credits themselves do not count as income for the purposes of calculating income. A single individual with no children could qualify for a maximum of $487 in tax credits, $3,250 with one child, $5,372 with two children, and $6,044 with three or more.[22] Louisiana's tax credit, for example, maps entirely onto the federal government's program and adds 3.5 percent to the amount the recipient receives from the IRS.[23]

Temporary Aid to Needy Families (TANF)

On August 22, 1996, President Clinton signed into law the Personal Responsibility and Work Opportunity Reconciliation Act of 1996 (P.L. 104–193), which goes under the acronym PRWORA. PRWORA went into effect the following year on July 1, 1997, when the federal program Aid to Families with Dependent Children (AFDC) officially converted into Temporary Aid to Needy Families (TANF, pronounced tan-iff), a federal program that is partially funded with matching funds by the federal government and partially funded and administered in the respective states. When people speak of "welfare," TANF is the program to which they are typically referring. It is far and away the largest program in income assistance both in terms of the number of recipients and also in terms of program costs. It is also, unquestionably, the most politically contested program in the American social safety net.

AFDC was a means-tested entitlement program, which means that if one qualified on the basis of income and assets owned, an adult could be on the program indefinitely—as long as they had qualifying children. AFDC came under attack for three reasons. First, critics argued that the policy created incentives for being on welfare as a lifestyle, and impressive quantities of ink were spilled on both sides researching the validity of this statement. Second, many governors and members of Congress (along with President Clinton, who had served as the governor of Arkansas) argued that AFDC was too inflexible, uniform, and unresponsive to local needs and that if they were provided with some freedom to spend funds in innovative ways, the states could create more effective programs to get recipients into the labor market. A third argument was coupled to the second and called for freedom to experiment as a good in itself, allowing the states once again to serve as "laboratories of democracy." This appeal to federalism was based more in the realm of theory, giving the calls to change AFDC more of a theoretically appealing underpinning. For some combination of these reasons, in 1996 AFDC was converted into TANF with the support mostly of Republican members of Congress and the Democratic President Bill Clinton, ending the entitlement aspect of AFDC. Through waivers allowing them exemptions from various federal requirements, states also now have the latitude to experiment with programs such as offering subsidized daycare or public transportation, for example, or to try different versions of workforce development. As with other federal programs they administer, states are also free to call TANF by other names. In Missouri it is simply called "Temporary Aid" (TA), while in Massachusetts, TANF goes under the name Transitional Aid to Families with Dependent Children (TAFDC). It is called the Family Independence Temporary Assistance Program, "FITAP," in Louisiana, and CalWORKs in California.[24]

While TANF is categorized here as an income support program, it comes with significant other benefits, especially medical benefits, as well as assistance for burial expenses, transportation assistance, help with finding employment, and, depending on the state, subsidized childcare so parents can go to work and even a clothing allowance for uniforms of safety gear. There are structural incentives in the way states are reimbursed by the federal government to get recipients working as fast as possible, for parents to get or remain married, and also to keep families from having more children.[25]

The changes in the program's name from Aid to Families with Dependent Children to Temporary Aid to Needy Families are very telling, and the word "families" in both is very important. Households must have dependent children, or the wife must be at least five months pregnant.[26] Moreover, the word "temporary" is also quite meaningful. Federal law prevents an adult recipient from being on TANF for longer than two years at a time (children can be on until they reach twenty in Massachusetts, nineteen in Texas and Louisiana), and not more than five years over their lifetime, although the two-year limit can be extended if a member of the family is over sixty-five, if the parents and dependent teens are all in school, if a member of the household becomes disabled, or if a member of the household is in the final 120 days of a pregnancy. Otherwise, after being on the program for two years, an adult cannot re-apply for five. States have the option of extending benefits using their own funds, as Missouri does, for example, allowing recipients ninety-day renewable extensions.[27] Immigrants are also ineligible for the first five years they are in the country from TANF benefits using federal funds, with the exceptions of "refugees, asylees, an alien whose deportation is being withheld, Cuban/Haitian entrants, Amerasians, and veterans, members of the military on active duty, and their spouses and unmarried dependent children."[28] States, however, are allowed to provide TANF benefits to immigrants in the first five years using their own funds exclusively. As of 2009, sixteen states, including California, did this, and another six states provided benefits to children and some to battered spouses.[29]

All adults in a household on TAFDC must be working or looking for work, and indeed, if all children are over nine years old in Massachusetts (six in Texas), all adults must either be working at least thirty hours per week, be enrolled as students or in a training program or internship, or be performing community service. All children must be enrolled and attending school, and families with children who skip school will see their benefits cut. In Texas, guardians can be exempted from the work rules if they are: (a) ill or incapacitated or caring for someone who is; (b) are sixty or over, or; (c) have a child less than a year old.[30] Families that do not comply can lose their TANF benefits, and also "food stamps," now known as SNAP (Supplemental Nutrition Assistance Program) and even Medicaid eligibility (both SNAP and Medicaid are discussed below).[31]

CalWORKs

Since every state is slightly different, the easiest thing to do is walk through one state in detail, and then afterward we will see each of the five states in comparison. For our example, we will look at the benefits available to a poor household in Los Angeles. Once again, in California, TANF goes by the name CalWORKs, and the programs are administered locally by the fifty-eight county welfare departments. Benefits come at two levels depending on the cost of living in the given county, and Los Angeles County is considered a high-cost county.

As all state TANF programs do, since they are funded by the federal government that mandates them, CalWORKs has four stated purposes. First, assisting needy families so that children can be cared for in their own homes. Second, reducing the dependency of needy parents by promoting job preparation, work, and marriage. Third, preventing out-of-wedlock pregnancies. Finally, CalWORKs must encourage the formation and maintenance of two-parent families.[32] This articulation of the mission of TANF makes it clear that while income support is the primary purpose, it is not the sole mission, and this helps explain why the program is so work oriented. Indeed, a key element of the program is that in households that are receiving funds from CalWORKs, the adults in the household must either be working or seeking work. A single parent must engage in thirty-two hours per week of work, training, or job search activities. A two-parent household must engage in thirty-five hours per week. There are exemptions for pregnant women with complications that prevent them from working, single parents with a child under the age of one, adults who are disabled or who cannot work for medical reasons, and parents who are aged sixty or over, plus those who are caretakers for another household member who is ill or incapacitated. All children on CalWORKs must be in school. Adults who do not comply with the work rules (which fall under the Welfare to Work, or WTW, program) will lose their portion of the funding.[33]

To be eligible for CalWORKs, each individual applying must be a United States citizen or lawful immigrant, and a resident of California. The household income must fall below the limits found in Table 2.2 below. Additionally, the household cannot have more than $2,000 in liquid assets ($3,000 if the parents are sixty or over), and, as mentioned above, parents must participate in the Welfare To Work activities. Children need to have received their immunization shots and must attend school on a regular basis. Household vehicles must be valued at $4,650 or less ($8,500 in Kansas[34]), homes are exempted from the asset limits, and families may set aside up to $5,000 in restricted accounts to save up for a down payment on a home, or to start a business or pay for educational expenses. Finally, families in CalWORKs must have child support payments sent through the California Child Support Services Department, which will keep the payments, passing on $50 to the family. If the household does not cooperate with child support, they will have their TANF support cut by 25 percent.[35]

Table 2.2 Maximum Weekly Payments under CalWORKs, by Family Size[36]

Family Size	Maximum Aid Payment (Non-exempt)	Maximum Aid Payment (Exempt)
1	$ 351	$ 317
2	$ 577	$ 516
3	$ 714	$ 638
4	$ 849	$ 762
5	$ 966	$ 866
6	$1,086	$ 972
7	$1,192	$1,069
8	$1,301	$1,164
9	$1,405	$1,258
10+	$1,510	$1,351

To calculate how much a household will receive per week under Cal-WORKs, the first step is to calculate the household's income that will be counted. The California Department of Social Services (DSS) is going to look at three categories of income: (1) earned income; (2) unearned income; and (3) disability income. A *disregard* is a fixed amount or a percentage of income that is not counted as "income." (We saw this above when looking at Unemployment Insurance.) Finally, there is income that is not even counted—although DSS still requires that it be reported—and this is referred to as "exempted" income.

Earned income, as the name implies, comes from employment, be it a salary or wage, a commission, or income from a business the individual owns. It can also be for "in-kind" work, such as when one provides service at, say, a daycare center in return for having one's child enrolled there instead of paying tuition. Earned income has a $112 weekly disregard and then after that 50 percent of the remaining is also disregarded. So someone working twenty hours a week at $9 an hour would have $180 in gross income. Then she would need to calculate earned income by calculating the disregards:

$180 − $112 = $68
$68 * .5 = $34

Thus, this individual would have $34 in earned income per week.

Unearned income is income that is neither earned nor comes from being disabled. Social Security survivor's benefits, child support, income from investments, or retirement benefits, for example, would all be counted as unearned income. There is no disregard for unearned income, so any income coming in is counted directly against one's CalWORKs benefit (except, as noted above, the first $50 of child support if paid through Child Support Services).

Disability Income comes from the social safety net, such as Worker's Compensation, a parent's Social Security Disability Insurance (SSDI) benefits, private disability insurance, and California state disability insurance, and no other forms. There is a $225 weekly disregard for disability income, so that if one were receiving, say, $400 a week from Worker's Compensation, $175 of that would be counted against the CalWORKs benefit.

To figure out how much a household will receive in a week, one then totals all the income after the disregards and subtracts that from the Maximum Aid Payment, found in Table 2.2. The "exempt" column is used if all of the household income comes from disability payments made to adults.[37] Thus, going back to our example of the single parent working twenty hours a week at $9 an hour, if he or she had one child, that household would receive ($577 − $34 = $543) per week, if the parent were somehow exempted from having to work at least thirty hours as required.[38]

California Welfare to Work

As noted above, all adult CalWORKs recipients must work at least thirty-two hours per week if they are single, or a combined thirty-five hours per week for a couple, while they are receiving benefits. There are exceptions (which are extensive and are listed in the endnote).[39] Those who are in the Welfare to Work program and residing in Los Angeles will be able to partake in the service of LA GAIN (Greater Avenues for Independence), which offers a wide range of courses to help program participants find fruitful employment.[40] LA GAIN also reaches out to employers and holds job fairs where those looking for future employees can connect with CalWORKs recipients, in order to make the hiring process more direct and easier. LA GAIN works with LA LINK, another program of the Los Angeles Department of Social Services. LA LINK is another employment service that subsidizes the employee search costs of businesses by providing free job posting services, free pre-screening, and free computerized matching services and human staffing specialists.[41]

Cal-Learn[42]

Cal-Learn is a program for pregnant and parenting teenagers on CalWORKs, who have not yet completed high school. These participants receive transportation and childcare support, and work intensively with a social worker to ensure that they graduate from high school, as doing so counts towards their Welfare to Work requirement. Students with a C grade or higher can receive an additional $100 once per quarter as a bonus, which will not be counted as earned income.

California Tribal TANF Program (CTTP)[43]

On July 8, 2003, California established the California Tribal TANF Program (CTTP), which is now associated with thirty-five Native American tribes in the state. Households with children who are members of any of the participating tribes can receive the same services as any other California resident seeking CalWORKs benefits, only they can participate in programs that are based locally (often on tribal lands) and administered through CTTP, allowing them to remain within their own culture and to be served by those who are respectful of it. As with teenagers elsewhere, young recipients are eligible for a wide range of programs focusing on pregnancy prevention, healthy relationships, communication and sexual decision making, negotiating skills, individual and group counseling sessions, and also programs such as one entitled "Learning from Our Tribal Elders."[44]

Summary

TANF, as described above for California, is more than just an income support system. As we shall also see below when we look at Houston, participation in

TANF renders one eligible for medical benefits, SNAP benefits ("food stamps"), and a range of benefits from childcare subsidies to job placement assistance to support for travel expenses and even purchasing tools or uniforms for work.

General Relief (GR)[45]

California allows its counties to provide assistance to the needy as it deems fit. All counties offer the program, although some call it General Assistance. In Los Angeles County it is called General Relief (GR). GR is aimed at helping indigent adults who live alone and have no income or financial resources. The following categories of individuals are eligible for assistance:

- Employables are participants with no medical conditions that would prevent employment. GR employables may receive GR for nine months in a twelve-month period, provided they continue to comply with GROW requirements.
- Employable with Accommodations is assigned to individuals who are employable, but need certain accommodations in order to work or have certain limitations/restrictions in the type of work they can perform.
- Unemployables are participants who have one or more medical conditions (temporary or permanent) affecting their ability to work. GR benefits are not time limited for unemployables.
- Unemployable with Accommodations is assigned to individuals who are unemployable, but volunteer to participate in GROW.
- NSA means Need Special Assistance and is the identification of individuals who need special assistance due to a mental disability.
- Administratively Unemployable means there are reasons other than physical or mental incapacity which prevent the individual from finding, accepting, or continuing existing employment.

GROW stands for General Relief Opportunities for Work, and is similar to the Welfare to Work and accompanying LA GAIN programs discussed above.[46]

TANF across the States

The benefits available to poor households vary from state to state. Table 2.3 shows the maximum amount available to a household in each of the five cities.

TANF in Texas

Since TANF is more than just an income support program, and given the ability of states to innovate, it makes sense to look at what is offered under TANF in more than just one location. Having studied CalWORKs as implemented in Los Angeles, we can look at TANF in Houston.

Table 2.3 Maximum Benefits from TANF, by State and Household Size

# in Household	Boston[47]	Houston[48]	Kansas City, KS[49]	Los Angeles[50]	New Orleans[51]
1	$ 428	$ 113	$224	$ 351	$122
2	$ 531	$ 235	$309	$ 577	$188
3	$ 633	$ 271	$386	$ 714	$240
4	$ 731	$ 326	$454	$ 849	$284
5	$ 832	$ 362	$515	$ 966	$327
6	$ 936	$ 416	$576	$1,086	$366
7	$1,037	$4,351	$637	$1,405	$402
8	$1,137	$ 514	$698	$1,510	$441

In Texas, the Texas Workforce Commission (TWC) offers a range of free workshops for job seekers from how to create a résumé to learning how to use a computer so as to apply for positions online, to dealing with stress and creating a financial plan, just as we saw above in looking at Massachusetts. To start, any adult receiving assistance through Temporary Aid to Needy Families in Texas must sign a Personal Responsibility Agreement[52] in which they pledge to:

- participate in the Choices program (unless exempt);
- cooperate with child support requirements;
- not voluntarily quit a job;
- have their child(ren) screened through the Texas Health Steps (THSteps) program;
- have their child(ren) immunized;
- have their child(ren) attend school;
- attend parenting skills training if referred; and
- not abuse drugs or alcohol.

Just as a side note, an agreement such as this is found in every state, and in Missouri, it has an interesting side effect. Applicants cannot have more than $1,000 in assets (other than a home and car) until the "self-sufficiency pact" is signed, after which they can own $5,000.[53] Those who fail to follow the pact will receive only a maximum of 25 percent of the eligible payments.[54]

The Texas Choices Program[55]

All states have a work requirement, but in Texas more than in the other states we examine, work is presented more prominently to its TANF recipients, who learn that the state follows what is known as a "work first" model, meaning that adults on TANF must search for employment, and accept any offer that pays reasonably close to their old wages. Once they have applied for TANF, applicants are required to attend a Workforce Orientation for Applicants seminar, where they will learn about available services offered by the TWC. Afterward, recipients will have an individual Employment Planning Session and meet with a social worker to develop a job search plan and review how the services discussed in the Workforce Orientation might help them find full-time employment. Single parents are expected to work at least thirty hours per week, two-parent households fifty-five hours a week, but this also includes time spent on job searches, including writing résumés, and taking courses on self-esteem building, interviewing techniques, and retaining job skills.[56] Exceptions can be made to the work requirement for victims of spousal abuse and in cases where the adults cannot obtain childcare. One can only spend so much time on these, however, and those who do not find employment after four weeks will have to provide community service. In return, they will receive assistance with childcare and transportation, and other work-related expenses.[57] While the state of Texas wants its TANF recipients to work, it does not want them to be in a position where they are perversely incurring expenses in the process of doing so.

Recipients who find employment may also still qualify for benefits. One difficulty that many leaving TANF encounter is that their work-related expenses (especially childcare) can be so high that they can end up with less while working than when they were not. Thus, under the Texas Choices program, recipients may qualify for continuing assistance with childcare, transportation, and other job-related expenses (such as, again, paying for uniforms), and the Choices staff will also help recipients learn about and apply for other support services and benefit programs.[58] (California, in fact, allows former CalWORKs recipients to retain their childcare benefits for up to two years as long as they remain employed.)[59]

Skills Development Fund[60]

The goal of the Skills Development Fund is to ensure that workers are being trained in positions that are in demand. Employers contact the TWC about what kinds of workers they need, and then develop partnerships with technical and community colleges that design programs to produce workers with those skills.[61] From the perspective of someone being retrained, this program is not visible, but it increases the likelihood that a school is offering a program in a field where Texas employers are hiring, hopefully resulting in training programs that actually meet the needs of both local employers and students. This is used in conjunction with the Self-Sufficiency Fund Program.

Self-Sufficiency Fund Program[62]

Anyone receiving TANF, SNAP or who is the parent of a child on CHIP (Children's Health Insurance Program, described in Chapter 5) is eligible to take courses at Texas technical or community colleges for free, care of funding from the federal Self-Sufficiency Fund Program, in order to adapt their skill set to the needs of the employment market. Moreover, the educational institutions offering these courses can receive funds to offer free childcare and even medical care (if it is on-the-job training), liberating parents to focus on their education.

Texas Veterans Leadership Program[63]

Texas does not provide benefits to veterans that other assistance recipients cannot receive, but it places veterans at the head of the line for some of them. Veterans, especially veterans of Iraq and Afghanistan, get priority treatment at TWC centers, and are allowed to apply for jobs posted by the state of Texas for two days prior to the postings being released externally. Veterans also benefit from a website that holds virtually all services offered by the state on one convenient webpage.[64]

Texas Back to Work Program[65]

The state of Texas provides financial incentives to employers to hire out-of-work Texans. If an employer hires an unemployed Texan who previously earned less than $15 an hour and retains that individual for at least four months of full-time work, the state will reimburse that employer $2,000.

One-Time TANF Payments[66]

Texas has set up a program where recipients get one lump sum payment and then cannot re-apply for a year. Families must meet the normal TANF income and asset requirements, and get a one-time payment of $1,000 in order to off-set a "short-term crisis" such as a job loss, a medical emergency, or the loss of child support. Grandparents can also qualify for a one-time payment, if they meet the same requirements and the grandchild living with them is on TANF.

Summary

What we see by looking at these programs is the very close relationship between the public and private sectors. State governments must get certain percentages of their TANF populations back into the workforce in order to retain their federal funding, and to do so, states have gotten quite active in working with both training programs on the one hand and employers on the other to ensure that TANF recipients are equipped with the skills local employers need. The public and private sectors actually work rather closely in many programs, although this is frequently not seen by the public. Moreover, TANF gives states quite a bit of leeway in how they choose to implement their programs, so that in some states, the focus will be very heavy on job training, while in others, it may be on subsidizing, for example, childcare costs, since they can easily cost a parent more per hour to care for a child than she can earn in an hour. On that last note, one criticism of AFDC was that parents often lost benefits when they went back to work, meaning that they could actually be worse off financially by working full-time than being on welfare. By extending healthcare or other benefits for a year or two after the TANF participant goes back to work, this helps mitigate that problem, creating incentives (as expensive for the government as they may be) for individuals to return to employment.

Programs in Other States

As mentioned above, federalism allows states to serve as "laboratories of democracy," in which experiments not only allow localities to tune programs to the specific needs of their residents, but also to see what works and what does not. TANF is the perfect example of this, with programs varying, not always all that widely, but varying nonetheless. Below, we see some twists on the programs discussed in Massachusetts and Texas above, allowing readers to see differing approaches to the same issues.

Louisiana Kinship Care Subsidy Program (KCSP)[67]

Most of the discussion of Texas and Massachusetts TANF programs referred to children and parents, or to households. The Kinship Care Subsidy Program will fund households as long as the adults caring for eligible children are part of an extended family, thus increasing the range of households that are eligible to receive FITAP (again the Family Independence Temporary Assistance Program, as TANF is called in Louisiana). Louisiana, however, makes a distinction between children living with natural parents and children living with other adult caregivers. To qualify for TANF, parents must earn at or below 200 percent FPL. Adult caregivers who are not parents can qualify for KCSP if they meet all the qualifications for FITAP but fall below 150 percent of the Federal Poverty Line. The adult must also have been out of prison for at least one year if they have been convicted of a drug-related felony, and must be a legal guardian or have provisional custody of the child. Along with FITAP, applications can be filed in person or on paper sent to a local Economic Stability Office, or via the internet.[68] There will be a follow-up interview in person.

Louisiana Child Care Assistance Program (CCAP)[69]

Louisiana makes funds available for FITAP recipients to have their childcare expenses covered by the state in order to allow them to work or receive training. Children must be under thirteen, unless disabled, in which case they can be as old as eighteen. The amount of money available depends on household size. Gross income must fall below the limits listed in Table 2.4. If eligible, the state will pay the care provider directly.

Table 2.4 Monthly Gross Income Limits to be Eligible for Childcare Support, by Household Size, Louisiana[70]

Household size (persons)	Monthly gross income limit
2	$2,060
3	$2,545
4	$3,030
5	$3,515
6	$4,000
7	$4,090
8	$4,182
9	$4,272

Head Start

Head Start is a federal program administered by Health and Human Services to protect preschool children from the cognitive, physical, and emotional effects of poverty. While one must be a resident of the state in which one is applying, migrant workers can also have their children admitted. The main qualification is an income below 133 percent FPL.[71]

As with many of the other programs listed in this section, Head Start can also be viewed as a basket of goods. The Louisiana State Head Start Collaboration Project (LSHSCP), for example, takes a comprehensive approach to caring for needy pre-literate children in a manner that both integrates the parents into the process and also seeks to ensure that there are as few "gaps and overlaps in service delivery" as possible.[72] The main element of Head Start is ensuring children are in a daycare system that provides them with a safe and secure environment for them to develop, and families in Head Start are expected to contribute to the learning environment when possible through their participation. Children receive free medical and dental examinations, there are nutrition seminars for the parents, and the family receives free access to social workers who ensure that the household gets all the possible benefits for which it qualifies.[73] Head Start has broad national reach, with there being close to forty providers in just New Orleans alone.[74]

Supplemental Security Income (SSI)

Those who are permanently disabled and unable to support themselves and who have virtually no assets can apply for Supplement Security Income (SSI), a federal program that is administered by the Social Security Administration but funded from general revenue and not from Social Security taxes. To be eligible, one must be legally blind or disabled, or over the age of sixty-five, plus be a U.S. citizen or a qualified alien,[75] and have less than $2,000 for an individual or $3,000 if a couple in countable assets, including cash and investments, land, and other easily liquidated assets other than one's home, one vehicle, household goods and personal effects, life insurance and burial funds valued at less than $1,500, wedding rings, and grants or scholarships for education.[76] Supplemental Security Income does not count the first $20 in monthly income from any source, nor the first $65 per month earned from working, and only half of income over that is counted as well. It will also not count SNAP benefits, shelter provided by non-profits, or most home heating assistance.[77]

Across the nation, SSI recipients are automatically eligible for SNAP benefits as well. Massachusetts and California supplement SSI with a State Supplemental Program (SSP), which in Massachusetts is linked seamlessly so that beneficiaries need only apply for SSI and the additional benefits come automatically. This is not true for all states. Some administer their benefits separately (as Louisiana, Missouri, and Texas do), while Arizona, North Dakota, the Northern Mariana Islands, Mississippi, and West Virginia do not supplement benefits at all.[78] In Louisiana, the state supplements SSI by $8 per person per month.

Cash Assistance Program for Immigrants (CAPI)

Because SSI and California's SSP are largely walled off for many immigrants due to federal laws, California has created its own program using only state funds to assist certain elderly, blind, and disabled legal immigrants who otherwise would be eligible for SSI or SSP, except for their immigrant status. CAPI participation also helps these individuals obtain benefits from Medi-Cal, In-Home Supportive Services, and SNAP. Individuals must apply at the local county General Relief office.[79] The California Department of Social Services has put together a table to show the payments, comparing SSI and CAPI, in Table 2.5.

Social Security Disability Insurance

SSI is a means-tested disability program. Recipients do not need to have ever worked so much as one day in their lives to receive benefits—which of course, makes sense for a program aimed at the disabled. Social Security Disability Insurance (SSDI) is a program for those who have been in the working world and contributed to Social Security, and who are either totally disabled and are hence unable to engage in "successful gainful activity" for a period that is estimated to be longer than twelve months, or who have a terminal illness. An individual cannot receive benefits until having been disabled for five months, although the application process is so long that it will take longer than that to make one's way through it anyhow.[80]

Table 2.5 Payment levels for SSI/SSP and CAPI[81]

SSI/SSP and CAPI Payment Levels

Individuals

	7/11		1/12		1/13	
	SSI	CAPI	SSI	CAPI	SSI	CAPI
Aged/Disabled	$ 830.00	$ 820.40	$ 854.40	$ 844.40	$ 866.40	$ 856.40
Disabled Minor	$ 737.40	$ 727.40	$ 761.40	$ 751.40	$ 773.40	$ 763.40
Blind	$ 885.00	$ 875.40	$ 909.40	$ 899.40	$ 921.40	$ 911.40
Board and Care	$1,086.00	$1,076.00	$1,110.00	$1,100.00	$1,122.00	$1,112.00

Couples

	7/11	1/12	1/13
Both SSI/SSP			
Aged/Disabled	$1,407.20	$1,444.20	$1,462.20
Blind	$1,554.20	$1,591.20	$1,609.20
Aged/Disabled & Blind	$1,498.20	$1,535.20	$1,553.20
Both CAPI			
Aged/Disabled	$1,387.20	$1,424.20	$1,442.20
Blind	$1,534.20	$1,571.20	$1,589.20
Aged/Disabled & Blind	$1,478.20	$1,515.20	$1,533.20
One CAPI, One SSI			
Aged/Disabled	$1,397.20	$1,434.20	$1,452.20
Blind	$1,544.20	$1,581.20	$1,599.20
Aged/Disabled & Blind	$1,488.20	$1,525.20	$1,543.20

This program is aimed at protecting those who cannot work but previously did, and is structured to encourage the injured to get back to work. Of course, not all injuries or illnesses are of the nature where one day one cannot work and the next day one is fully healed, so SSDI is structured in a manner that allows workers to generate some income in the process of healing, without automatically losing all of their benefits. In 2013, workers were able to earn up to $750 a month without losing their benefits. A recipient could earn between $750 and $1,010 a month and be considered to be performing "services," which they could do for up to nine months in any sixty-month rolling period (blind people could earn up to $1,690 a month instead of $1,010). If a worker performs "services" for more than nine months, or earns more than $1,010 in a month, their benefits would terminate, but could start up again any time for thirty-six months after the last payment if the worker's earnings declined again due to the illness.[82]

Emergency Aid to Elders, Disabled and Children (EAEDC)[83]

Even with TAFDC, SSI, and SSDI, there are still households that for one reason or another will not be able to get benefits, although they are unable to earn an income due to disability. In order to catch these people in the welfare safety net, the Commonwealth of Massachusetts created Emergency Aid to Elders, Disabled and Children (EAEDC), administered by the Department of Transitional Services. The beneficiary must either be disabled or be the caretaker of someone who is. In order to be eligible, one must have applied for SSI and either be waiting to hear back from the Social Security Administration, or have already been rejected. The recipient must also be ineligible for TAFDC.

To be eligible for EAEDC, one must either be a U.S. citizen or legal resident, and have a Social Security Number. Countable assets cannot be more than $250 per person or $500 per couple, including cash, bank accounts, savings, pensions and retirement accounts, stocks and bonds, cars, and real estate. In addition to the application, the beneficiary will be visited once a quarter by a social worker, and although there are no time limits for remaining on EAEDC, each case is formally reviewed twice a year.

As with SSI and SSDI, beneficiaries can have some income and still receive benefits, which are subtracted from the net income. Those able to work can subtract $90 per month for work-related travel expenses (such as bus fares), and are also able to deduct the first $30 they earn plus one-third of the remaining income (the "disregard") for four months, and if the remaining income is below the maximum allowable benefits (see Table 2.6), they can receive the difference. After four months, the "$30 plus one-third the disregard" deductions disappear and cannot be used again for another twelve months.[84]

Table 2.6 Maximum Monthly Benefits per Family under EAEDC[85]

Family Size	Maximum EAEDC Monthly Benefit
1	$303.70
2	$395.10
3	$486.60
4	$578.20
5	$669.80
6	$761.10
Each additional person	$ 91.60

Chapter 115 Benefits (formerly called "Veterans' Services")[86]

Just as EAEDC is a catch-all program for disabled individuals who for one reason or another do not qualify for another program, the Commonwealth of Massachusetts has created a program for veterans in dire need, entitled simply "Chapter 115 Benefits." This program is presented as a temporary program designed to run anywhere from six months to one year, with the goal of helping the veteran through a brief period of financial hardship and to get back on his or her feet, but in practice it can also help those medically unable to work indefinitely. For the able-bodied, the program is similar to TAFDC in that the income assistance is one element of the package—and a not-insignificant one—but the program's social workers will also work very hard to help recipients find other benefits and more importantly, to help them find gainful employment. The program is also open to spouses and children under nineteen (or under twenty-three if they are still attending college or another training program).

Chapter 115 is a joint state/local program where Massachusetts contributes 75 percent of the funds and the local town the other 25 percent, with programs being regulated by the state Commissioner of Veterans' Services. The program provides a monthly income ceiling of $1,210, and will subtract any income from other programs or retirement plans from that amount. Five to six hundred dollars of the monthly payment should go towards rent. The program will provide an additional $250 per month for fuel and utilities. Finally, the program will pay the individual's health insurance premiums, regardless of whether the insurance is from the private sector or a public program such as Medicare.

To be eligible, an applicant must have served for at least ninety days in the armed forces during wartime, including at least one day in combat, or have served at least one hundred and eighty days otherwise, and have not more than $2,000 in assets. Finally, the veteran should have an honorable discharge, and cannot be receiving benefits from other programs.

Childcare

DTA Child Care[87]

In Massachusetts, poor families, including all families on TAFDC, are eligible for free or subsidized childcare to help parents search for and retain gainful employment. Known as "DTA Child Care," funding is provided by the Department of Transitional Assistance, with the goal of getting parents back to work, and to that end, to be eligible, parents must be actively looking for work, employed, attending school, or be enrolled in a qualifying training program. The state Child Care Resource and Referral (CCR&R) agency negotiates "contracted slots" with many facilities in which the childcare center agrees to a lower rate per child, and in return the CCR&R guarantees payment for the slots whether they are filled or not. It then makes the slots available to DTA Child Care recipients. Otherwise, TAFDC households will get a voucher for free childcare at any facility, up to the amount of the voucher, which varies depending on the household's income.

Income-Eligible Child Care[88]

Poor households may still be eligible for assistance with costs even if they are not on TAFDC, as long as they are employed or looking for work, in school or a training program, are on maternity leave, or are disabled. How many hours of care a child will get and how much of a subsidy the state will pay is determined by family size and income, as calculated by a CCR&R counselor.[89]

Homeless Child Care

Homeless families placed in a shelter by a state agency are automatically eligible for childcare for all children under the age of twelve, or sixteen if they have special needs, for the times when the parents are looking for housing, in school or a training program, counseling sessions or parent training, or other approved activities offered by the shelter. Vouchers are extended for thirty days after the family leaves the shelter.[90] Families must meet the same income limits as those applying for Income-eligible Child Care.[91]

Child Support

One goal of PRWORA was to help parents with custody actually to obtain the child support owed them by the other parent. One element of the Act allows states to subrogate child support—that is, to have the other parent send the child support payments to the state instead of to the custodial parent in order to ensure the payments actually do get made. Each state also now maintains a computer system that tracks so-called "deadbeat" parents so that anyone who owes child support cannot simply leave town without being able to be found. States can garnish wages (although that is very expensive for them to do so), but more importantly, each state now has a mechanism for parents—especially parents on TANF—to help find individuals who owe them child support, along with legal mechanisms to help them obtain the back support they are owed.[92]

Conclusion

Income assistance can lift a household above poverty if the recipients were above poverty to begin with and stopped working due to the breadwinner getting injured. But this assistance will usually be for a short time only. For households that are forced to rely on TANF, the financial component will not bring them anywhere close to the Federal Poverty Line. That being said, we need to see TANF as more of a basket of goods—so much so, in fact, that most states automatically qualify households for SNAP benefits as well, just to make the benefits received more comprehensive. What we have also seen in this section is that the benefits a household receives under TANF can vary quite dramatically from state to state, both in terms of income assistance, and also in terms of other elements instead, such as subsidized childcare (perhaps extending years after the household leaves TANF), training assistance, and even help paying for public transportation and uniforms or tools needed for the new job.

We have also seen that income support programs are often pegged not merely to income, but also to assets owned. Other than money put aside in a home and a car, plus a burial plot (the government pays for that too, if a person dies indigent—more on that later), households are often limited to owning not more than two to three thousand dollars' worth of goods.

With this in mind, we can start to think about the multiple purposes of income support programs, and begin to see that some of them may be contradictory. On the one hand, at the very least, programs should provide the poorest with a roof over their heads, enough to keep them from starving, and provide them with the ability to accumulate enough in income and assets to facilitate a rise from poverty. From another angle, households simply cannot have enough in income or assets ever to rise out of poverty while on these programs. That of course is by design, in order to encourage households to find employment that will allow them to rise through working. Can most households on TANF or the other programs find the kind of work that will pay them enough to rise up the socioeconomic ladder? Instead, will they simply move from dead-end unskilled job to unskilled job? In the latter, are these programs really about getting participants to rise out of poverty, or are they more about getting them off the rolls? This is a highly political question, but one that needs to asked in earnest, since there are many ways these programs can be designed, and the choice of options can have a dramatic impact on the lives of those within them.

When AFDC was converted to TANF in the mid-1990s, states responded with a range of innovations, and we now have had two decades to study how those different policies have played out. For our purposes, what we have seen in this chapter is that the line between the public and the private sectors is not as clear-cut as might have been expected. Texas has done a remarkable job of *facilitating* market forces through bringing training schools and employers together in order to allow for as much information to be exchanged as possible, allowing technical schools to understand where the demand is in terms of what kinds of skilled employees are in or will be in demand by local employers.

Likewise, Texas and other states have come to realize that sometimes the biggest impediments to individuals accepting job offers is the inability to find affordable daycare, which, again, can easily cost more per hour than many people have the capacity to earn. One option, obviously, is simply to pay more in TANF benefits, but that is often politically unacceptable, while subsidizing childcare, even if the costs are no different, is a policy that is able to find its way to passage through state houses. Thus, policy making is not simply about which policy works the best, but more often than not about which one works the best within the political confines of the polity.

Notes

1   The best resource of Unemployment Insurance is the Department of Labor's website: http://www.dol.gov/dol/topic/unemployment-insurance/index.htm. For Massachusetts, see http://www.mass.gov/lwd/unemployment-insur/, for Texas, http://www.twc.state.tx.us/ui/unemployment-benefits-services.html (accessed August 2013).
2   http://www.twc.state.tx.us/ui/bnfts/claimant1.html (accessed August 2013).
3   http://www.twc.state.tx.us/ui/bnfts/claimant1.html. To see how benefits are calculated in detail, see http://www.twc.state.tx.us/ui/bnfts/bi-99.pdf#calculate (accessed August 2013).
4   For comparison, in Louisiana, benefits range from $10 to $247 per week, for a limit of six months. www.laworks.net/Downloads/UI/UIBenefitRightsInformation.pdf (accessed August 2013).
5   http://www.edd.ca.gov/unemployment/Eligibility.htm (accessed August 2013).
6   http://www.edd.ca.gov/unemployment/Forms_and_Publications.htm#de1275a (accessed August 2013).
7   http://www.twc.state.tx.us/ui/bnfts/claimant1.html. It should also be noted that there are exceptions for those who could not earn due to illness, injury, or pregnancy.
8   http://www.twc.state.tx.us/ui/bnfts/claimant3.html (accessed August 2013).
9   A portion for farmers was modified in 2002 under P.L. 107–210, Sec. 141, allowing farmers to apply if their loss of income was due to declines in commodity prices caused by imports.
10   For a broad overview, see http://www.twc.state.tx.us/svcs/taa/trade-adjustment-assistance-program-overview.html (accessed August 2013).
11   http://workforcesecurity.doleta.gov/unemploy/tra.asp (accessed August 2013).
12   http://www.irs.gov/individuals/article/0,,id=187948,00.html (accessed August 2013).
13   For Texas, see http://www.tdi.texas.gov/wc/employee/index.html. For Massachusetts, WC is administered by the Massachusetts Executive Office of Labor and Workforce Development, Division of Industrial Accidents (DOI).
14   http://www.dol.ks.gov/WorkComp/current.aspx (accessed August 2013).
15   http://www.dol.ks.gov/WorkComp/injwkr.aspx (accessed August 2013).
16   http://www.military.com/benefits/veteran-state-benefits/state-veterans-benefits-directory.html?comp=7000023431425&rank=5 (accessed August 2013).
17   http://www.calvet.ca.gov/VetServices/OtherBenefits.aspx (accessed August 2013).
18   http://www.vetaffairs.la.gov/Programs/Benefits.aspx (accessed August 2013).
19   http://www.military.com/benefits/veteran-state-benefits/missouri-state-veterans-benefits.html (accessed August 2013).
20   http://www.military.com/benefits/veteran-state-benefits/texas-state-veterans-benefits.html (accessed August 2013).

21   http://www.military.com/benefits/veteran-state-benefits/massachusetts-state-veterans-benefits.html (accessed August 2013).

22   http://www.irs.gov/Individuals/EITC-Income-Limits,-Maximum-Credit--Amounts-and-Tax-Law-Updates (accessed August 2013).

23   http://www.dss.state.la.us/index.cfm?md=pagebuilder&tmp=home&nid+162&pnid=158&pid=11 (accessed August 2013).

24   Temporary Aid in Missouri is administered by the Family Support Division of the Missouri Department of Social Services. TAFDC in Massachusetts is administered by the Department of Transitional Assistance inside the Executive Office of Health and Human Services. FITAP in Louisiana is administered by the Louisiana Department of Children and Family Services (DCFS), formerly the Department of Social Services. TANF in Texas is administered by the Texas Health and Human Services Division, and by the Office of Family Assistance under the Kansas Department of Health and Human Services. The California Department of Social Services administers CalWORKs.

25   Perhaps the most important is that 90 percent of work-eligible adults must be either working, training, or engaged in other forms of job search activities, or that given state may lose portions of its federal block grant. http://fcpe.adelphi.edu/Social_site/TANF.htm (accessed August 2013).

26   Obviously, there are many children who are cared for by someone other than their parents. Other adults who are eligible to receive TANF benefits in their role as caretakers of eligible children are stepparents, grandparents, siblings (including stepbrothers and sisters), aunts and uncles, nieces and nephews, and first cousins, including first cousins once removed.

27   http://www.dss.mo.gov/fsd/tempa.htm (accessed August 2013).

28   Testimony of Wade F. Horn, Assistant Secretary for Children and Families, U.S. Department of Health and Human Services before the Ways and Means Committee, U.S. House of Representatives, July 26, 2006. http://www.hhs.gov/asl/testify/t060726.html (accessed August 2013).

29   http://aspe.hhs.gov/hsp/11/ImmigrantAccess/Eligibility/ib.shtml#fig2 (accessed August 2013).

30   http://www.hhsc.state.tx.us/Help/Financial/temporary-assistance.shtml (accessed August 2013).

31   http://www.dss.state.la.us/index.cfm?md=pagebuilder&tmp=home&pid=92 (accessed August 2013).

32   www.lao.ca.gov/handouts/health%2f2012/recent_history_CalWORKs_2_29_12.pdf (accessed August 2013).

33   http://www.ladpss.org/dpss/CalWORKs/wtw.cfm (accessed August 2013).

34   http://www.tanf.us/kansas.html (accessed August 2013).

35   http://www.ladpss.org/dpss/CalWORKs/eligibility.cfm (accessed August 2013).

36   "CalWORKs: How Much Should I Get? (Region 1)" http://www.google.com/url?sa=t&rct=j&q=&esrc=s&source=web&cd=1&cad=rja&ved=0CDMQFjAA&url=http%3A%2F%2Fwww.lsnc.net%2Ffact_sheets%2Fcw_region_1.pdf&ei=7U2ZUJ7ePKHz0gGRmoHIBg&usg=AFQjCNF8B1KSKSLAAdWbdKrARNNgP5LYXQ&sig2=YQLaRE11FSk-E06V2aYWOg (accessed August 2013).

37   "CalWORKs: How Much Should I Get? (Region 1)" http://www.google.
com/url?sa=t&rct=j&q=&esrc=s&source=web&cd=1&cad=rja&ved=
0CDMQFjAA&url=http%3A%2F%2Fwww.lsnc.net%2Ffact_sheets%2Fcw_
region_1.pdf&ei=7U2ZUJ7ePKHz0gGRmoHIBg&usg=AFQjCNF8B1KSKSL
AAdWbdKrARNNgP5LYXQ&sig2=YQLaRE11FSk-E06V2aYWOg (accessed
August 2013).

38   N.B. One challenge faced by many poor individuals with little to no skills is
that employers do not want to hire the unskilled for more than twenty hours
per week in order to avoid having to provide them with benefits. Thus, many
individuals who have to meet the weekly work requirement must do so by
holding two or more part-time jobs.

39   Adults who do not have to meet the work requirement are among the following:
Caretaker relatives who are not the parent and are not aided; Individuals
caring for ill or incapacitated household members; Parents or caretakers aged
sixty and older; Pregnant women whose condition prevents involvement in
work activities; Single parents caring for a child under one year of age, and;
Participants who are disabled or have a medical excuse. There are also a series
of "good cause" reasons that may also exempt an individual or household from
the work requirements: An individual needs supportive services that are not
currently available; The participant is ill, or caring for a sick member of the
family; Childcare is not reasonably available for a child under ten years of age
during the participant's hours of training or employment, including travel time;
A breakdown or interruption in childcare occurs; The participant is a victim of
domestic violence and participation is detrimental to or penalizes the participant
or family; Discrimination exists in terms of age, sex, race, religion, national origin,
or physical or mental disability; The conditions involved are in violation of health
and safety standards or do not provide worker's compensation; Round-trip travel
time is in excess of two hours or two miles when walking is the only means of
transportation; The activity would cause the individual to violate the terms of
union membership; The hours of participation exceed the daily or weekly hours
customary for that job; Accepting the job or work activity would interrupt the
participant's approved job or training program already in progress.

40   http://www.ladpss.org/dpss/gain/default.cfm (accessed August 2013).

41   http://www.ladpss.org/dpss/lalink/default.cfm (accessed August 2013).

42   http://www.ladpss.org/dpss/CalWORKs/calearn.cfm (accessed August 2013).

43   http://www.cttp.net/index.html (accessed August 2013).

44   http://www.cttp.net/services.html (accessed August 2013).

45   http://www.ladpss.org/dpss/gr/default.cfm (accessed August 2013).

46   http://www.ladpss.org/dpss/grow/default.cfm (accessed August 2013).

47   http://www.massresources.org/pages.cfm?contentID=17&pageID=
4&subpages=yes&dynamicID=353 (accessed August 2013).

48   http://www.hhsc.state.tx.us/Help/Financial/temporary-assistance.shtml
(accessed August 2013). This is for households with one parent. If there were
households of the same size but with two parents, the amount decreases.

49   http://content.dcf.ks.gov/ees/keesm/Appendix/F-4_TAFtable07_11.pdf
(accessed August 2013).

50 http://ca.db101.org/ca/programs/income_support/CalWORKs/program2b. htm (accessed August 2013).

51 http://www.dss.state.la.us/index.cfm?md=pagebuilder&tmp= home&nid=109&pnid=7&pid=139&catid=0 (accessed August 2013).

52 http://www.dads.state.tx.us/handbooks/texasworks/A/2100/2100.htm (accessed August 2013).

53 http://www.dss.mo.gov/fsd/tempa.htm (accessed August 2013).

54 http://www.dss.mo.gov/fsd/tempa.htm (accessed August 2013).

55 http://www.twc.state.tx.us/welref/choices-program-overview.html (accessed August 2013).

56 Louisiana makes it very clear that those who choose not to work may not only lose their TANF income, but be cut off from the SNAP and Medicaid programs as well. [http://www.dss.state.la.us/index.cfm?md=pagebuilder&tmp=home&pid=92] (accessed August 2013).

57 http://www.twc.state.tx.us/welref/choices-program-overview.html (accessed August 2013).

58 Louisiana actually spells out some of the possible expenses that might be covered: childcare, transportation, eyeglasses, hearing aids, medical exams and drug tests that are required for employment, uniforms and clothing, safety equipment, tools, and certain other items needed for work or training. http://www.dss.state.la.us/ index.cfm?md=pagebuilder&tmp=home&pid=92 (accessed August 2013).

59 http://www.dss.cahwnet.gov/getinfo/faq/faqsprogram.html (accessed August 2013).

60 http://www.twc.state.tx.us/svcs/funds/sdfintro.html (accessed August 2013).

61 For the Workforce Investment Act in Texas, see http://www.twc.state.tx.us/boards/ wia/workforce-investment-act-program-overview.html (accessed August 2013).

62 http://www.twc.state.tx.us/svcs/funds/ssfintro.html (accessed August 2013).

63 http://www.twc.state.tx.us/svcs/vetsvcs/veterans-services-program-overview. html (accessed August 2013).

64 http://www.twc.state.tx.us/tvlp/tvlp.html (accessed August 2013).

65 http://www.setworks.org/TBTW.aspx (accessed August 2013).

66 http://www.hhsc.state.tx.us/Help/Financial/temporary-assistance.shtml (accessed August 2013).

67 http://www.dss.state.la.us/index.cfm?md=pagebuilder&tmp=home&pid=138 (accessed August 2013).

68 https://cafe-cp.dcfs.la.gov/selfservice/ (accessed August 2013).

69 http://www.dss.state.la.us/index.cfm?md=pagebuilder&tmp=home&pid=136 (accessed August 2013).

70 http://www.dss.state.la.us/index.cfm?md=pagebuilder&tmp=home&pid=136 (accessed August 2013).

71 http://www.benefits.gov/benefits/benefit-details/1913 (accessed August 2013).

72 http://www.dss.state.la.us/index.cfm?md=pagebuilder&tmp=home&pid=61 (accessed August 2013).

73 http://www.dss.state.la.us/index.cfm?md=pagebuilder&tmp=home&pid=61 (accessed August 2013).

74 http://eclkc.ohs.acf.hhs.gov/hslc/HeadStartOffices#map-home (accessed August 2013).

75   A "qualified alien" is someone who falls into one of seven categories: Lawfully admitted for permanent residence, Granted conditional entry under Section 203(a) (7) of the Immigration and Nationality Act (INA) as in effect before April 1, 1980; Paroled into the U.S. under Section 212(d)(5) of the INA for a period of at least one year; Refugee admitted to the U.S. under Section 207 of the INA; Granted asylum under Section 208 of the INA; Deportation is being withheld under Section 243(h) of the INA as in effect before April 1, 1997, or removal is being withheld under Section 241(b)(3) of the INA; "Cuban or Haitian entrant" under Section 501(e) of the Refugee Education Assistance Act of 1980 or in a status that is to be treated as a "Cuban/Haitian entrant" for SSI purposes; or if the applicant, spouse, or child has been subjected to certain forms of battery while in the United States (http://www.socialsecurity.gov/ssi/text-eligibility-ussi.htm) (accessed August 2013).

76   http://www.socialsecurity.gov/ssi/text-resources-ussi.htm (accessed August 2013).

77   http://www.socialsecurity.gov/pubs/11000.html#part5 (accessed August 2013).

78   http://www.socialsecurity.gov/ssi/text-benefits-ussi.htm (accessed August 2013).

79   http://dpss.lacounty.gov/dpss/capi/default.cfm (accessed August 2013).

80   In addition, around 60 percent of applications are initially denied. http://www.disability-benefits-help.org/content/about-ssdi (accessed August 2013).

81   http://www.dss.cahwnet.gov/shd/res/htm/SSItables.htm (accessed August 2013).

82   http://ssa-custhelp.ssa.gov/cgi-bin/ssa.cfg/php/enduser/popup_adp.php?p_faqid=317&p_created=959362523 and http://www.socialsecurity.gov/OACT/COLA/twp.html (accessed August 2013).

83   http://www.massresources.org/pages.cfm?contentID=16&pageID=4&Subpages=yes (accessed August 2013).

84   "106 CMR: Department of Transitional Assistance," Chapter 321. http://wwhelp.wwrc.net/wwwebhelp/eaedc_membership_in_the_assistance_unit_and_filing_unit_massachusetts.htm (accessed August 2013).

85   http://www.massresources.org/pages.cfm?contentID=16&pageID=4&subpages=yes&dynamicID=345 (accessed August 2013).

86   http://www.mass.gov/veterans/benefits-and-services/chapter-115.html (accessed August 2013).

87   http://www.massresources.org/pages.cfm?contentID=25&pageID=8&subpages=yes&dynamicID=478 (accessed August 2013).

88   http://www.massresources.org/pages.cfm?contentID=26&pageID=8&Subpages=yes (accessed August 2013).

89   For a current eligibility table, see: http://www.massresources.org/pages.cfm?contentID=26&pageID=8&subpages=yes&dynamicID=489#financial (accessed August 2013).

90   http://www.massresources.org/pages.cfm?contentID=133&pageID=8&Subpages=yes (accessed August 2013).

91   For a current eligibility table, see: http://www.massresources.org/pages.cfm?contentID=26&pageID=8&subpages=yes&dynamicID=489#financial (accessed August 2013).

92   More information on Massachusetts can be found at: http://www.mass.gov/dor/child-support/ (accessed August 2013).

Chapter 3

Housing Assistance

One major challenge faced by poor households is finding safe and affordable housing. In rural areas, there may not always be an adequate quantity of rentable housing stock. In urban areas, housing may be available but not affordable. The federal and local governments (states rarely play much of a role in this area) help to subsidize the costs of finding adequate residences through one of three basic categories. The first are tenant-based vouchers, in which the recipients find housing on the private market, and the government helps them pay the rent. The second category is the reverse of the first, in which in the government subsidizes landlords directly in return for them charging below-market rates for their rentals, which the households pay for on their own. Finally, there is public housing, where the government itself owns and operates the housing, and charges below-market rates for it. We will talk about each of these in turn.

Tenant-Based Voucher Programs

Housing and Urban Development Vouchers

By far and away, the largest form of helping poor households with housing is through the use of vouchers. The main program is operated jointly between a given locality and the U.S. Department of Housing and Urban Development (HUD). The largest program is the Housing Choice Voucher Program (HCVP), which was formerly known as the Section 8 voucher program[1] and one often still sees it referred to in this manner, as in the state of California. The purpose of the HCVP is to assist very-low-income families, the elderly, and the disabled in obtaining "decent, safe, and sanitary housing in the private market."[2] Recipients can use a voucher to help pay the rent at any privately owned apartment, single-family house, townhouse, or condominium, with the household paying no more than 30 percent of their monthly adjusted income in rent. The voucher will pay for the remainder of the rent (which can be no more than 70 percent of the household's monthly adjusted income), up to the fair market rent of the housing unit.[3] In other words, a household is limited to a rental costing not more than their entire adjusted monthly income, of which, again, they will pay 30 percent. Family size will determine how many bedrooms the residence can have.[4] The program is in theory open to any household earning less than 80 percent of the area's median income (AMI), allowing the program some flexibility across localities, but the federal law underpinning the program is specifically designed to help those at the very bottom of the income bracket, and mandates that at least 70 percent of the vouchers go to households earning less than 30 percent of the area's median income. As we can see from Table 3.1, eligible income varies quite widely. A family of three residing in Houston could have an income of no greater than $15,050 to qualify at 30 percent of the AMI, but the same household in Kansas City could have an income as high as $19,250.

The voucher program is a popular option among participants because it gives households the chance to choose the specific type and location of their residence.[5] Houston and New Orleans both provide approximately 17,000 vouchers, Boston 11,000, Los Angeles 47,000.

In any event, this is all academic since the program is frozen in all the localities under study except Kansas City, and none of the others are taking in new applications, not even for the waitlist.[6] Indeed, New Orleans has 17,000 vouchers but a waitlist of 20,000.[7] To be eligible for a Housing Choice voucher, the household must have at least one member who is living in the country legally, and none of the members can possess a conviction for a violent crime or a drug offense in the last three years, owe any money to their local housing authority or HUD, and must not have been evicted from any federally funded program in the last three years. The head of household must be over eighteen years old, unless they are emancipated minors.[8]

Programs Available to Poor Households in Boston, MA

Specific programs vary from city to city, and for housing, we will go into detail about the programs available to poor households in Boston.

Massachusetts Rental Voucher Program (MRVP)[9]

These vouchers work just like federal Housing Choice vouchers, only are funded by Massachusetts and in Boston are administered through the Boston Housing Authority. To be eligible to apply, applicants must have incomes under 200 percent FPL.[10] Looking at Table 1.1, this means that a single individual cannot not earn over $22,980 per year, while a family of three could not earn more than $39,060. Households will not pay more than 30 to 40 percent of their adjusted gross income for rent, and at least one member must be a United States citizen. The household must also be able to provide good references and cannot have any serious criminal history. As with the Housing Choice Voucher Program, the MRVP is also not accepting new applicants.

Table 3.1 Maximum Allowable Household Incomes for Section 8 Vouchers, by Household Size[11]

Household Size	80% Boston AMI	30% Boston AMI	80% LA. AMI	30% LA. AMI	80% NO AMI	30% NO AMI	80% KC AMI	30% KC AMI	80% Houston AMI	30% Houston AMI
1	$47,150	$19,850	$46,400	$17,400	$33,800	$12,700	$39,900	$14,950	$31,200	$11,700
2	$53,900	$22,650	$53,000	$19,900	$38,600	$14,500	$45,600	$17,100	$35,650	$13,400
3	$60,650	$25,500	$59,650	$22,400	$43,450	$16,300	$51,300	$19,250	$40,100	$15,050
4	$65,000	$28,300	$66,250	$24,850	$48,250	$18,100	$56,950	$21,350	$44,550	$16,700
5	$67,350	$30,600	$71,550	$6,850	$52,150	$19,550	$61,550	$23,100	$48,150	$18,050
6	$72,750	$32,850	$76,850	$28,850	$56,000	$21,000	$66,100	$24,800	$51,700	$19,400
7	$78,150	$35,100	$82,150	$30,850	$59,850	$22,450	$70,650	$26,500	$55,250	$20,750
8	$88,950	$37,400	$87,450	$32,850	$63,700	$23,900	$75,200	$28,200	$58,850	$22,050

Family Self-Sufficiency Program (FSS)[12]

The FSS, also known as the Housing Choice Family Self-Sufficiency Program, is not a voucher program, but rather an additional program for households on Housing Choice vouchers to assist them in obtaining long-term independence. FSS social workers help households on vouchers to find childcare, education, job training, substance abuse counseling, household skill training, transportation to work and, notably, homeownership counseling. To be eligible, the head of the household must be employed and no member can be on Temporary Aid to Families with Dependent Children, as, recall, TANF is called in Massachusetts. The individual or family meets with a counselor and set up goals for the next five years. If their incomes increase, their rent does not, and the difference goes into an FSS bank account to be used for one of the goals listed in the contract.[13]

In Houston, the HHA strives to make tenants into owners by selling many of their single-family properties through the Historic Homeownership Program. To partake in this program, a household must earn between 60 to 80 percent of the Houston Area Median Income (AMI), which, looking to Table 3.1, would be no more than $31,200 for a single individual and $40,100 for a family of three.[14] The Housing Authority of New Orleans (HANO) has been rebuilding many of its housing projects that were destroyed or damaged by Hurricane Katrina under a new model under which many of the units are privately owned so as to create mixed-use communities.[15]

California has two programs to help families whose incomes fall below 80 percent of AMI and who are first-time homebuyers purchase their own homes: the Down Payment Assistance (DPA)[16] program, and the Home Ownership Program (HOP).[17] DPA, as its name implies, is intended to help the poor who cannot accumulate enough for a down payment by providing them with the lesser of either 6 percent of the purchase price, or $10,000. HACoLA places a lien on the property, and when it is sold or the mortgage is refinanced, the money is then paid back. HOP is not available everywhere. If in the proper area, a buyer can obtain a zero percent loan of up to $35,000 or 25 percent of the purchase price, making it easier for the household to obtain financing for the rest of the mortgage amount. As of the time of writing, neither program was taking applications.

MassHousing

MassHousing is a state-operated bank that offers housing loans to low- and moderate-income Massachusetts residents at sub-market rates. It also has a counseling service for first-time homebuyers and renters, to help them find housing they can afford. MassHousing also operates the Tenancy Preservation Program, which will litigate on behalf of those threatened with eviction due to mental illness, age-related impairments, or substance abuse problems.[18]

There are also numerous other programs targeting specific constituencies.

- Conversion Vouchers are for families dislocated by the destruction of their homes or the gentrification of their neighborhoods.
- Family Unification Vouchers are for families that would have to split up due to inadequate housing.
- Homeownership Vouchers are for poor families to become homeowners rather than having to rent all their lives. These programs typically have the household work with a case manager to create a five-year plan where they create a budget, and any increases in income do not result in an increase in rent, but instead are placed in an escrow account, and at the end of the five-year period will serve as part of the down payment on a home, as with FSS.[19]
- Eviction Grants are typically one-off payments for families in immediate danger of being evicted due to an uncontrollable financial event that is surmountable with a small amount of financial assistance, provided in part through federal and in part local funds. In Houston, for example, households can apply to local charities for these grants, and the charities themselves interact with the Houston Housing Agency. The Housing Assistance Program of Greater Kansas City (HAP) runs the Medical Crisis Rental Program, aimed at keeping the employed who are at risk of becoming homeless due to medical reasons in their homes. For those who were working for at least forty-five days prior and are now unemployed due to a medical condition, and have no other sources of income, HAP can provide up to three months of rent or mortgage payments, plus utilities.[20]
- Homeless Prevention and Rapid Re-Housing Program (HPRP).[21] The federal government and various states and localities also provide funds to prevent homelessness by helping individuals and households with motel vouchers, rent and utility payments, legal representation and counseling, and even bus tickets to other locations where there may be jobs or family.[22] In Los Angeles, 4,000 HCVP vouchers are reserved for homeless individuals and households that have been referred to HACLA by other agencies.[23] Kansas City took the program (known as Kansas City Project Hope) in another direction, providing rental and utility assistance or motel vouchers, for up to eighteen months, to those who are homeless or about to find themselves in that condition, outside of the HCVP system.[24] Benefits can only last for eighteen months, and beneficiaries must have an annual income of not higher than 50 percent of Kansas City's AMI. Unlike the voucher program, participants may receive up to 100 percent of housing costs (including motel vouchers for up to thirty days), along with other social services, a case manager to help them find both housing or to help them rectify their financial situation, and legal assistance if it appears they are being evicted illegally.[25]
- Housing and Urban Development Veteran Affairs Supportive Housing Vouchers (HUD-VASH Vouchers) for veterans. This program is aimed at preventing homelessness, providing vouchers for one year, in

combination with other services such as theory and case management at the nearest Veterans Affairs medical center.

- Welfare-to-Work Vouchers give temporary assistance while families transition from being fully dependent on welfare to securing and maintaining a job, helping them to become self-sufficient.
- Alternative Housing Voucher Program (AHVP). This is specifically for disabled individuals under the age of sixty. Again, residents will pay not more than 30 to 40 percent of their adjusted gross income in rent, and at least one member of the household must be a U.S. citizen.[26] Household income must be below 80 percent of the median income of the city or town.
- Housing Opportunities for People with AIDS (HOPWA). Many people diagnosed with HIV and AIDS cannot find housing, and HUD created a program administered through local non-profits where they build housing and rent it out, usually coupled with provision of health and psychological services.[27] In Houston, for example, TEXT MSG (Teaching Empowerment to Exit Transitional Housing by Managing Secure Goals) is a program aimed at eighteen- to twenty-four- year-olds with HIV/AIDS who have been chronically homeless. The goal is to find them their own apartments and provide them with the therapy and social services to get them employed and independent.[28]
- Vouchers for the Elderly and Disabled. In part due to the wait needed to find subsidized housing, the Boston Housing Authority (BHA) has created a special program for the elderly and disabled. The BHA maintains a list of HUD approved private housing appropriate for the impaired, and keeps separate waitlists for studios and one bedroom apartments, with another for two bedroom apartments. Applicants are ranked according to need, with priority being factored into those who are displaced by fire, domestic violence or eviction, time on waitlist, veteran status, being a resident of Boston, and being aged sixty-two or over.
- Witness Relocation Vouchers.[29] For individuals who are cooperating with law enforcement about crimes that occurred in or around public, Indian, or other HUD-assisted housing, this program provides them with Section 8 vouchers that can allow them to move from the perpetrators. Note that these vouchers can be used to help the members of the household move anywhere in the nation, not simply across town.

Low Income Housing Energy Assistance Program (LIHEAP)

Sometimes the poor have so little income that they have to make choices between heating or cooling their homes and paying for other goods, such as food or other necessities. The Low Income Housing Energy Assistance Program, or LIHEAP, is intended to help the poor pay for their utility bills. The federal government is the primary source of funding for this program, with states making additional contributions if they desire. To be eligible for

Table 3.2 LIHEAP Income Thresholds for Los Angeles[30]

Number of Members in Household	Gross Income Threshold
1	$24,304
2	$31,782
3	$39,260
4	$46,738
5	$54,216
6	$61,694
7	$63,096
8	$64,498

LIHEAP assistance in Los Angeles, one's gross income must be no more than 60 percent of the area's median income, which for L.A. is found in Table 3.2.

In Los Angeles, LIHEAP recipients will see their electricity, sewer, and water bills reduced by up to 15 percent in addition to financial support for paying the utility costs. They can also apply for a second program, California Alternative Rates for Energy (CARE), funded by a utility surcharge on other customers, which will lower electricity and natural gas costs by 20 percent. Those who qualify for CARE can also receive other benefits as well, such as assistance for weatherizing one's home, repairing or replacing non-functioning heating systems, and even purchasing more energy-efficient heating systems and large appliances like refrigerators.[31] California's Department of Community Services and Development also has a pilot project where one thousand low-income families had photovoltaic solar systems installed on the roofs of their homes at no cost.[32]

Any household on SNAP or TANF is automatically eligible for LIHEAP. A program that connects SNAP and LIHEAP ("Heat and Eat") will be discussed below.

Voucher Programs for Landlords

The programs just discussed were targeted at the poor households themselves, mostly allowing them to go onto the housing market and find a residence of their own choosing, which is made affordable through assistance from the government. The programs listed in this section instead target the landlords, who approach HUD or the local housing authority instead of the tenants doing so. Why use one form of voucher versus another? As we shall see below, some landlords own so many properties that it is simply easier for them to fill out the paperwork and get the payments directly, rather than rely on their tenants (who may not be as reliable in filling out paperwork) to do so. Some programs allow for funding to continue even when there are no tenants, allowing for a steady income stream. Finally, some are seen as providing an incentive for landlords to convert their property to affordable housing, or even to purchase vacant houses and convert them into affordable housing.

Moderate Rehabilitation Program[33]

This program provides the vouchers not to the households, but rather to the landlords, in return for providing below-market rent. We can think of housing-based vouchers as the government subsidizing the private housing market so it can offer affordable housing to low-income households. It does this by paying landlords the difference between below-market prices and what they could actually get on the open market. The federal government does this through Section 8 vouchers, while Massachusetts, for example, does this through a different part of MRVP. This program could be used by a land-lord with a three-family house, or an apartment building, or a former hotel that could cater to those at the very bottom of the socioeconomic spectrum. As with the HCVP, these programs also have long waits and few vouchers are available in proportion to those eligible, so much so in fact that current estimates are that an eligible applicant would be on a waitlist for about ten years in Boston.[34]

HUD allows a local public housing authority to allocate up to 20 percent of its HCVP vouchers to be used towards Project-Based Vouchers.[35] Private landlords contract directly with the local public housing authority (PHA), often on a long-term basis, and the private rentals serve, in effect, as public housing units, allocated by the PHA. When a family moves out, the contract remains, and a new family allocated through the PHA moves in. This has the benefit of virtually guaranteeing the private landlord a long-term income, and allows the PHA to provide housing without owning the units itself.

In 2000, the mayor and city council of Los Angeles created the Affordable Housing Trust Fund, which provides below-market loans to developers of low-income housing.[36] In 2012 there were two rounds of loans from the fund, the second lending out ten million dollars in financing.

Single Room Occupancy Program (SRO)[37]

The SRO is a federal program set up under the McKinney-Vento Homeless Assistance Act, and is operated by the local housing authorities in order to help homeless individuals. Under the program, landlords must put at least $3,000 into rehabilitating housing, which they must then rent out to home-less individuals. Recipients must pay 30 percent of their income in rent, with the SRO paying the rest. Many shelters and The Ys (as YMCAs are now called) offer single rooms under this program, allowing individuals with limited incomes the ability to have a place of their own—literally just one room—that is still safe, clean, and affordable.

Public Housing

Each of the five localities owns and operates public housing, as summarized in Table 3.3.

Table 3.3 Housing Authorities and Public Housing

Agency Name	Number of Units	Number of Locations	Number Reserved for Elderly and Handicapped[38]	Approximate Number of Residents
Boston Housing Authority BHA[39]	14,000 units	63	36 for elderly (62 and older) and handicapped	27,000 residents
Houston Housing Authority HHA[40]	4,000 units and 200 single-family homes	25 public housing and tax credit developments	*	5,500 households
Housing Authority of Kansas City HACK[41]	1,900 units	25 sites, from high-rise apartments to townhouses	Around 400 units	*
Housing Authority of the City of Los Angeles HACLA[42] / Housing Authority of the County of Los Angeles HACoLA[43]	HACLA 6,528 units HACoLA 2,962 units	HACoLA 70 sites	*	HACLA 21,300 residents in over 6,500 households
Housing Authority of New Orleans HANO[44]	4,087 units administered, but only 2,532 are public; the rest are privately owned	HANO is in transition due to Hurricane Katrina. It is replacing larger projects with ten smaller mixed-income ones throughout the city[45]	*	5,000 families lived in public housing pre-Katrina, less than a third do so now

*No data available.

We can look to Boston and New Orleans to flesh out public housing. The Boston Housing Authority is the largest owner of housing in all of New England (indeed, including vouchers, the BHA houses 10 percent of the residents of Boston), operating sixty-three housing projects throughout the city. Of these, thirty-six are reserved for those aged sixty-two and over or disabled, with another twenty-four specifically for families with children. One of the elderly units has housing for families, and two of the family units have housing for the elderly and disabled.[46] The BHA maintains over 14,000 units that house over 27,000 people. The size of the apartment one can obtain is contingent upon the number of members of the household. Individuals under the age of twenty-five of the same gender must share a room, except that those over the age of fourteen are not required to share a room with someone under the age of ten.

In addition to meeting income limits, anyone in public housing that is supported by HUD must be a U.S. citizen or legal immigrant, and not have any violent or drug convictions in the last three years.[47] Systems also allocate places on the waitlist not simply by how long one has been waiting, but also via a points system. The more points one has, the higher on the waitlist one will be placed. Table 3.4 shows the points system for the Housing Authority of New Orleans.

New Orleans is, of course, a very special case, due to the lingering effects of Hurricane Katrina, a Category 3 hurricane that slammed into Louisiana the morning of Monday, August 29, 2005. Katrina destroyed over 70,000 units of affordable housing,[48] along with nearly a third of the city's public housing.[49] As a result of the city's residents fleeing the city due to the storm, the population of New Orleans experienced a 29 percent decrease from 485,000 in 2000 to 344,000 in 2010,[50] along with a 35 percent rise in rental costs.[51] The response has given the Housing Authority of New Orleans (HANO) the opportunity to pursue a new model of public–private ownership, which, as mentioned above, means housing developments where some of the properties inside of them are privately owned. Over time, public housing residents will have the opportunity to purchase the units they own as well. Due to a long history of corruption, HANO was taken over by HUD in 2002, and now private management firms oversee the operations of many of its units.

Table 3.4 Point Allocation for Public Housing, New Orleans[52]

Preference	Hours	Points
Working	30+	5
Elderly/Disabled	Exempted	5
Working	25 to 29	4
Working	20 to 25	3
Full-time Student	12+ credit hours	3
Working/ Job Training	20 < and in job training	2
Working	19 or less	1
Not Working	N/A	0

Homeless Shelters

There are, of course, also numerous homeless shelters operated by non-profit organizations, especially the Catholic Church, in every city, and some of these facilities are quite large, offering shelter for hundreds of individuals per night, usually associated with a soup kitchen. As mentioned, shelters can also be a source of Single Room Occupancy housing, described previously, charging not more than 30 percent of the individual's income for rent, while others offer dormitory-style sleeping arrangements. While shelters are operated by private, non-profit organizations, they typically have extremely close working relationships with the government agencies in the given city, often so strong indeed that their social workers based at the shelters can automatically qualify applicants for certain benefits, reducing redundancy on already stressed government social workers. Thus, although non-profits are not formally part of the government social safety net, they are a vital addition to it, often working seamlessly with state and local agencies to help those in need.

While the number of individuals served do not seem staggering, the costs of housing and providing social services for the homeless can be quite high, given the challenges presented—and of course, for those being provided with a roof over their heads, the impact can be profound. A quick look at Kansas City gives us a chance to reflect on what would happen were those shelters not there. ReStart, Inc. provides shelter for about one hundred single adults per night, on a first-come, first-served basis.[53] Founded after a homeless person froze to death outside in 1987, the Forest Avenue Family Shelter houses thirty-two women and children per night.[54] The Kansas City Rescue Mission provides rooms for seventy-six men per night, and serves meals to over 80,000 distinct individuals annually,[55] while City Union Mission had beds for 300 men and 121 beds for women and children, with another twenty-one rooms for longer-term stays.[56]

Summary

Poor households have a number of options theoretically open to them when it comes to housing. They can use vouchers to find housing on the private market, landlords can use vouchers to lower the rental costs, or families and individuals can apply for public housing. In practice, many of these options are closed due to lack of availability, but all strive to work in the same manner, which is to offer safe and decent housing that costs no more than 30 percent of total income, with the primary focus targeted to those in extreme poverty.

Interestingly, housing is often coupled with other social services, especially the provision of healthy meals. Homeless shelters are usually linked to soup kitchens that operate out of the same building, and as we shall see in Chapter 4, public housing projects often also have facilities to feed children who reside there and in the surrounding neighborhoods. We often also see childcare or Head Start programs operating out of public housing projects, allowing parents of young children to work, when they often have jobs that pay less an hour than most daycare facilities charge. Finally, we see that public housing, SRO operations (especially The Ys), and homeless shelters, often have social workers who help those receiving assistance find their way onto all the other programs for which they are eligible, in addition to finding stable work so they can lift themselves into better financial positions.

All that being said, in virtually every locality large and small, housing assistance is an area constantly under extreme stress. Public housing spaces are in great demand, often with waitlists literally as large as the number of units available. Housing authority websites will actually say that new applications (other than those for emergencies) are not being accepted, or that expected wait times are ten years. The massive housing projects of the past are widely seen as mistakes, since they cram too many extremely poor into too close a proximity, and were often built on the outskirts of the city, far from the grocery stores, public transportation, and jobs. It is interesting to note that when projects are refurbished, they are often radically redesigned to be more humane and attractive,[57] often accompanied by decreases in the density of residents.

Even vouchers—which are far more market based, allowing households more choice as to where to live and developers the ability to focus on rehabilitating blighted areas—are unable to meet the demand.

Notes

1 N.B. The name "Section 8" comes from the Housing Act of 1937, in which the vouchers were listed in the eighth section of the bill. When the housing bill is periodically updated, they remain in Section 8 to this day.
2 http://www.hud.org (accessed August 2013).
3 "Fair market rent" is determined by examining floor space and amenities of the unit in comparison with similar units in the neighborhood. For levels, see http://www.massresources.org/pages.cfm?contentID=3&pageID=2&subpages=yes&dynamicID=378#section8rent (accessed August 2013).
4 See Section 8.8 of "2009 Amended Administrative Plan for Section 8 programs" in http://www.bostonhousing.org/pdfs/LHS2009AdminPlanSection8.pdf (accessed August 2013).
5 Landlords are not supposed to be able to reject an applicant because they want to pay with a voucher, although they can legally reject an applicant if they do not like the applicant's payment history, credit rating, or criminal background. http://www.hakc.org/voucher_program/owner.aspx (accessed August 2013).
6 http://www.bostonhousing.org/detpages/hservices417.html#2 (accessed August 2013).
7 In 2009, the Housing Authority of New Orleans opened the application process for three days, and then closed it when the waitlist hit 28,000 (http://www.hano.org/housing/FAQ_HCVP.pdf) (http://npntrumpet.blogspot.com/2009/09/fair-housing-center-voices-grave.html) (accessed August 2013).
8 http://www.hakc.org/voucher_program/section_8_program_overview.aspx/ (accessed August 2013).
9 http://workworld.org/wwwhelp/rental_voucher_program_mrvp_overview_massachusetts.htm (accessed August 2013).
10 http://www.massresources.org/mrvp-ahvp.html#eligible (accessed August 2013).

11 To find data for a given area, use the following link. Start by entering the last two numbers of the year, and type the two-initial state code in at the end of the line. Thus, for Houston, one would enter: http://www.huduser.org/Datasets/ IL/IL13/tx.pdf (Kansas City is located in Wyandotte County [but is listed at the top of the spreadsheet under the city itself], Boston in Suffolk County, New Orleans in Orleans, and take note that Houston is located in Harrison County, not Houston County!) (accessed August 2013).

12 http://www.massresources.org/section8-fss.html (accessed August 2013).

13 http://www.massresources.org/section8-fss.html (accessed August 2013).

14 http://www.housingforhouston.com/housing-programs/housing-choice-voucher/ housing-choice-voucher-homeownership-program.aspx (accessed August 2013).

15 http://www.hano.org/communities.aspx (accessed August 2013).

16 http://www3.lacdc.org/CDCWebsite/linkit.aspx?id=5327 (accessed August 2013).

17 http://www3.lacdc.org/CDCWebsite/EHD/Programs.aspx?id=5324 (accessed August 2013).

18 https://www.masshousing.com/portal/server.pt?open=512&objID=240&&PageID =420&mode=2&in_hi_userid=2&cached=true (accessed August 2013).

19 As just mentioned above, in Boston the program goes under the name of the Family Self-Sufficiency Program (FSS), a.k.a Housing Choice Family Self-Sufficiency Program.

20 http://www.thehap.org/medical_crisis.html (accessed August 2013). An additional pre-condition is that the recipient must apply for a Section 8 voucher, which is interesting because the Housing Authority of Kansas City itself states that the average wait for a voucher is three years [http://www.hakc.org/voucher_program/how_to_apply.aspx] (accessed August 2013).

21 http://portal.hud.gov/hudportal/HUD?src=/recovery/programs/homelessness (accessed August 2013).

22 For Houston, see http://www.houstontx.gov/housing/hprp.html (accessed August 2013).

23 http://www.hacla.org/specialprograms/#homeless-program (accessed August 2013).

24 http://www.kcmo.org/idc/groups/public/documents/neighborhood communityservices/hprpfactsheet.pdf. See also, http://www.donbosco.org/centers/ family-support-center/kansas-city-project-hope-hprp.html (accessed August 2013).

25 http://www.kcmo.org/idc/groups/neighborhood/documents/neighborhood communityservices/hprpeligibilitydoc.pdf (accessed August 2013).

26 http://www.bostonhousing.org/detpages/hservices417.html (accessed August 2013).

27 http://www.dshs.state.tx.us/hivstd/hopwa/default.shtm (accessed August 2013).

28 http://portal.hud.gov/hudportal/HUD?src=/program_offices/comm_planning/ aidshousing/programs (accessed August 2013).

29 http://portal.hud.gov/hudportal/HUD?src=/program_offices/public_indian_ housing/programs/hcv/witness (accessed August 2013).

30 http://www.benefits.gov/benefits/benefit-details/1540 (accessed August 2013).

31 http://www.consumerenergycenter.org/home/your_energy_bill/assistance. html (accessed August 2013).

32 http://www.csd.ca.gov/Services/HelpPayingUtilityBills.aspx (accessed August 2013).

33 "Housing Services" http://bostonhousing.org/housing_services.html. See also, http://www.bostonhousing.org/pdfs/LHS2009AdminPlanSection8.pdf (accessed August 2013).

34 http://www.massresources.org (accessed August 2013).

35 http://portal.hud.gov/hudportal/documents/huddoc?id=DOC_9157.pdf (accessed August 2013).

36 http://lahd.lacity.org/lahdinternet/AffordableHousingTrustFund/tabid/126/ language/en-US/Default.aspx (accessed August 2013).

37 http://portal.hud.gov/hudportal/HUD?src=/hudprograms/sro (accessed August 2013).

38 Note that under Section 504 of the Rehabilitation Act of 1973, housing authorities are barred from discriminating against any person with disabilities in any program that receives federal assistance. They must provide reasonable accommodations, defined as "a change; exception; or adjustment to a rule, policy, practice, or service that may be necessary for a person with a disability to have an equal opportunity to use and enjoy a housing unit; access to an agency's facilities, activities or programs; or public and common-use spaces." http://www.housingforhouston. com/housing-programs/public-housing.aspx (accessed August 2013). Housing authorities do not need to provide entire special developments for those in need of accommodations, but typically find it logistically easier to do.

39 http://www.bostonhousing.org (accessed August 2013).

40 http://www.housingforhouston.com/housing-programs/public-housing.aspx (accessed August 2013).

41 http://www.hakc.org/ (accessed August 2013).

42 www.hacla.org (accessed August 2013).

43 The Housing Authority of the County of Los Angeles was founded in 1938, but due to mismanagement, it was placed under the Los Angeles Community Development Commission (LACDC) in 1982, wherein it still resides today. http://www3. lacdc.org/CDCwebsite/HM/Home.aspx (accessed August 2013).

44 http://www.hano.org/. See especially http://www.hano.org/our_story/fact_sheet. pdf (accessed August 2013).

45 http://www.hano.org/communities.aspx (accessed August 2013).

46 http://www.bostonhousing.org/housing_services.html (accessed August 2013).

47 See, for example, what Kansas City says: http://www.hakc.org/public_housing_ program/public_housing_overview.aspx (accessed August 2013).

48 N.B. Much of the housing that was lost took quite long to be replaced. Even six years later, in 2011, only a third of the lost housing had been rebuilt. http://www. nytimes.com/2011/02/04/opinion/04fr3.html (accessed January 16, 2014).

49 http://www.npr.org/templates/story/story.php?storyId=129448906 (accessed August 2013).

50 http://quickfacts.census.gov/qfd/states/22/2255000.html (accessed August 2013).

51 http://www.nytimes.com/2009/10/04/us/04housing.html?pagewanted=1 (accessed August 2013).

52 www.hano.org/home/agency_plans/ACOP_Plan_2011.pdf p.40 (accessed August 2013).

53 http://www.restartinc.org/shelter.htm (accessed August 2013).

54 http://forestavenuefamilyshelter.org/About_Us.html (accessed August 2013).

55 http://kcrm.org/who-we-are/annual-report/ (accessed August 2013).

56 http://www.cityunionmission.org/services/our-services. (accessed August 2013). Number of beds care of a conversation of June 19, 2012 with a generous staff member.

57 The Forest Green Townhouses of Houston are a perfect example of what clean, affordable housing can look like: http://www.housingforhouston.com/housing- programs/housing-developments/forest-green-townhomes.aspx (accessed August 2013).

Chapter 4

Nutrition Assistance

Nutrition assistance programs in America are structured around three main programs: the Supplemental Nutrition Assistance Program (SNAP), often referred to as "Food Stamps," the Women, Infants and Children program (WIC), and a variety of programs administered by local school systems and non-profits, funded mostly by the federal government's School Breakfast and School Lunch Programs. Especially as it pertains to keeping poor children fed, these three programs combined striving to ensure that children receive an adequate breakfast and lunch provided institutionally almost every day, year round, with wholesome food being purchased and cooked by their families at home for dinner as well. There are a number of other programs, some of which are designed either to supplement or complement these three.

Supplemental Nutrition Assistance Program (SNAP)

Created by the Food Stamp Act of 1964 and formerly known as the Food Stamp Program, the program was renamed in 2008 and is now officially called the Supplemental Nutrition Assistance Program (SNAP), although it is still officially referred to as Food Stamps in Missouri,[1] and goes by the name CalFresh in California.[2] SNAP is funded by the Federal Department of Agriculture and administered by the respective states. Recipients are given an Electronic Benefit Transfer (EBT) card, similar to a credit card, which they can use in stores and at farmers' markets to purchase any food but pet food, alcohol, or prepared foods, since recipients are expected to cook all meals from scratch at home.[3]

To apply for benefits, applicants must apply in person at offices located across the state in which that person is a resident (although some counties in California are experimenting with phone interviews or online applications instead), and bring proof of identity, proof of household income and expenses, have or be applying for a Social Security Number, and be residents of the state in which they are applying. Adults aged sixteen through fifty-nine who do not have infants must either be working at least twenty hours per week or register for the SNAP Food Stamp Employment and Training Program (FSET), and actively seek employment and accept it if offered. Adults eighteen to forty-nine without children must also take part in the SNAP Food Stamp Work Program (FS/WP), and cannot receive benefits for more than three months if not employed or in a training program.[4] Adults in the country illegally are not eligible, but their children may be, and illegal adults who are part of a household with legal residents must have their incomes counted toward the household's income.[5] Legal immigrants are eligible if they have resided in the country for at least five years.[6] All California recipients must be fingerprinted and provide two photos of themselves as well.[7] Texas limits adults without children to being on SNAP for just three months out of every three-year period, although that can be extended by three months.[8]

Recipients must also be poor. A household cannot have countable assets of over $2,000 (house and lot are not counted, vehicles are assessed according to a formula), while households with someone over age sixty or a disabled member can have assets of up to $3,250.[9] In California, in order to encourage an escape from poverty, the state no longer counts property, retirement funds, cash, stocks, or bonds towards eligibility if there is a child under eighteen years old in the household.[10] In Louisiana, households are exempt from these limits if they are also receiving SSI or FITAP or are enrolled in the Strategies to Empower People (STEP) program, as FS/WP is called there. They are not exempt if they have been found guilty of an Intentional Program Violation, a drug violation, failing to work if required, or are on strike.[11] Moreover, a household's monthly income cannot be over 130 percent of the Federal Poverty Line, with net monthly income below the 100 percent FPL (households with a pregnant woman or at least one child under the age of nineteen qualify at the 200 percent FPL level). See Table 4.1. Notably, if the only household income comes from programs such as SSI, TANF, and EAEDC, then families do not have to meet income limits. But if there is some earned income in the household, then the income from these programs is counted, and receipt of them may render a household ineligible for SNAP.

Table 4.1 Maximum Gross and Net Income for SNAP Eligibility, by Household Size, for the Lower 48 States[12]

People in Household	Monthly Gross Income, Standard	Monthly Net Income, Standard	200% FPL (Families with Children)
1	$1,211	$ 931	$1,915
2	$1,640	$1,261	$2,585
3	$2,069	$1,591	$3,255
4	$2,498	$1,921	$3,925
5	$2,927	$2,251	$4,595
6	$3,356	$2,581	$5,265
7	$3,785	$2,911	$5,935
8	$4,214	$3,241	$6,605

Table 4.2 SNAP Food Stamp Program Maximum Monthly Allotments[13]

People in Household	Maximum Monthly Allotment
1	$ 200
2	$ 367
3	$ 526
4	$ 668
5	$ 793
6	$ 952
7	$1,052
8	$1,202
Each additional person	+$ 150

Net income is defined as 80 percent of gross income plus a deduction of $149 households with one to three members, $160 for four, $187 for five, and $214 for six or more members. There are also some allowable deductions for medical expenses.[14]

The idea behind SNAP is to provide adequate nutrition for each member of the household, based on the Thrifty Food Plan, which is a low-cost model diet plan created by National Academy of Science. Shoppers are anonymously sent to local grocery stores with a shopping list to price items, from which the maximum allotment found in Table 4.2 is calculated. To determine how much a recipient will receive, 30 percent of their net income is deducted from the maximum, since recipients are expected to spend one-third of their incomes on food (in addition, as we learned in Chapter 3, to spending one-third of their income on housing).

Looking to Tables 4.1 and 4.2, we see that a family of four with a monthly net income of $1,800 (roughly $21,600 in net annual income) qualifies for $128 in monthly SNAP food stamps.

Maximum allotment for a family of four	$668
Subtract 30 percent of net monthly income (.3 ★ $1,800)	$540
Monthly household food stamp benefit	$128

Heat and Eat (H-EAT)[15]

One challenge faced by certain households is that their heating bills are part of their rent, and since utilities are deducted when calculating net income, some households appear to have lower utility expenses than they really do, and their SNAP benefits are cut because of it.[16] To deal with this, some states allow LIHEAP participants to deduct automatically the maximum amount allowed under the deduction calculations, meaning that participating in LIHEAP may lead to higher benefits under SNAP.[17] This is called "Heat and

Eat" (or some close variation) by participating states. Interestingly, one must only receive a dollar in LIHEAP benefits in order to deduct the maximum standard utility allowance (or SUA, which is the term for the utility deduction) for SNAP, and this is notable because while that one dollar may come from state funds, SNAP comes entirely from federal funds, which is a way for a state to ensure that its residents receive the highest possible SNAP benefits funded by the federal government.

Combined Application Process (CAP)

Because they often live alone and are less mobile than others, and can find themselves challenged to deal with online applications, low-income seniors are the most likely to suffer from food insecurity. To make applying as easy as possible, a small number of states have implemented a Combined Application Process, or CAP, under the cooperation of the Department of Agriculture's Food and Nutrition Service (FNS, which administers all of the other programs listed here), the Social Security Administration, and local state agencies.

For residents of New Orleans, Louisiana, the program is called LaCAP. The applicant must be sixty or over, qualify for SSI, either be living alone or with people who do not prepare the applicant's food, cannot have any recent drug convictions, or be under accusation for an Intentional Program Violation.[18] In Massachusetts, sometimes referred to as the "Bay State" for the large bay inside Cape Cod, the program is called Bay State CAP. Interestingly, applying through CAP as opposed to directly to SNAP may allow some applicants to receive more support, but if the applicant has "high shelter costs, medical expenses, dependent care expenses, or child support payments, [they] might get higher benefits with regular SNAP food stamps."[19] This is, to this author's knowledge, the only instance where an applicant for a benefit may get more by applying through one venue than through another. The other three cities under study do not currently have CAP programs.

Farmers' Markets Programs

In an attempt to bring fresh produce to low-income families, states are now using their own funds to supplement SNAP, allowing SNAP participants to use part of their funds to make purchases at farmers' markets. In Missouri and Kansas, for example, the Beans and Greens program allows Kansas City SNAP beneficiaries to take up to $25 of their SNAP cards (called the Vision Program in Kansas and the Quest Program in Missouri), and Beans and Greens will match those funds dollar for dollar, if used at a participating farmers' market.[20] Thus, a participant can take $25 off of their Quest card, and use the $25 dollar match to purchase $50 worth of produce. Moreover, the Beans and Greens program maintains mobile trucks that carry produce to areas that lack farmers' markets.[21]

Women, Infants and Children (WIC)

The Special Supplemental Nutrition Program for Women, Infants, and Children (WIC) is designed to ensure that young children and their parents receive the necessary nutrition they need to develop in a healthy manner. It is jointly operated by the U.S. Department of Agriculture and the respective states, which operate the educational components of the programs. WIC is designed for pregnant women or women who have had a child within the last six months, or a year if still breastfeeding, and children up to the age of five. Foster children under the age of five automatically meet the income requirement. In addition to being impoverished, applicants must be at "nutritional risk," which may mean "a poor diet, weight problems, problems during pregnancy, food allergies, vitamin or mineral deficiencies, anemia, or other problems."[22] See Table 4.3.

Table 4.3 Louisiana Women, Infant and Children (WIC) Program Participants Qualifying Medical Condition for Special Formula[23]

Participant Category	Qualifying Medical Conditions
Infants (up to twelve months)	• Premature birth • Low birth weight • Failure to thrive • Metabolic disorders • Malabsorption syndromes • Immune system disorders • Life-threatening disorders, diseases and medical conditions that impair ingestion, absorption or utilization of nutrients that could adversely affect the participant's nutrition status
Children (up to five years of age)	• Premature birth • Failure to thrive • Metabolic disorders • Malabsorption syndromes • Immune system disorders • Life-threatening disorders, diseases and medical conditions that impair ingestion, digestion, absorption or utilization of nutrients that could adversely affect the participant's nutrition status
Women	• Metabolic disorders • Gastrointestinal disorders • Malabsorption syndromes • Immune system disorders • Life-threatening disorders, diseases and medical conditions that impair ingestion, digestion, absorption or utilization of nutrients that could adversely affect the participant's nutrition status

Table 4.4 Maximum Allowed Annual Income to Qualify for WIC[24]

Household Size	Maximum Annual Income
1	$21,257
2	$28,694
3	$36,131
4	$43,568
5	$51,005
6	$58,442
7	$65,879
8	$73,437
Each additional member of household	+$ 7,437

Table 4.5 Average Monthly WIC Benefits per Person, by State[25]

State	Average WIC Benefit
California	$49.35
Kansas	$40.03
Louisiana	$51.94
Massachusetts	$40.83
Texas	$29.30

A household cannot have an income above 185 percent FPL (see Table 4.4), but it should be noted that anyone who has qualified for SNAP or TAFDC automatically qualifies for WIC, if they meet the other requirements. Applicants must be interviewed in person and bring proof of residence and identification, along with proof of income, although documentation from SNAP or TAFDC will suffice.[26] They must also, of course, bring proof that they have qualifying children. Despite these qualifications, the program is massive. Approximately 54 percent of all U.S. infants and 25 percent of all U.S. children aged one to five benefit from this program.[27]

WIC is far stricter than SNAP in what its funds can be used to purchase. For example, recipients can use their WIC EBT card[28] to purchase milk, but only fat free, or wholegrain bread, but not white, and brown rice, but again, not white.[29] In order to make shopping easier, there are now stores in California—Mother's Nutritional Center stores[30] and Prime Time Nutrition in Oakland—that cater to the needs of WIC recipients by only stocking items that can be purchased through the program. Increasingly, WIC participants are able use their EBT cards at farmers' markets as well.[31]

The dollar value of WIC varies from state to state, as can be seen in Table 4.5. In certain other states, participants do not get EBT cards but rather packages of food. In 2003 the National Academies' Institute of Medicine suggested servings to ensure that "the food packages align with the Dietary Guidelines for Americans and infant feeding practice guidelines of the American Academy of Pediatrics," also taking into account various ethnic preferences to ensure that not only are the packages healthy, but that they are also desirable.[32] The contents are also aligned to how much the mother is breastfeeding.

> The food packages for breastfeeding infant-mother pairs provide incentives for continued breastfeeding. For example, the food package for fully breastfeeding women provides greater amounts of foods, including a higher dollar value for fruits and vegetables. Fully breastfeeding infants receive baby food meats in addition to greater amounts of baby food fruits and vegetables. Less infant formula is provided to partially breastfeeding infants so that they may receive the benefits of breastmilk. A minimal amount of infant formula is provided to partially breastfeeding infants in the first month after birth in order to help mothers build and maintain their milk production.[33]

It is important to understand that administrators do not see WIC as merely a supplement to SNAP, and instead envision the educational programs as being quite central, indeed fundamental, to the program. New Orleans, for example, has three WIC sites where participants have access to nutritionists and nurses, and WIC provides a range of classes for recipients, from proper breastfeeding to shopping on a budget to preparing healthy meals with classes on nutrition and the basics of healthy eating, all with the goal of getting households into the position of eating *healthy* food on a routine basis.[34] Recipients can also learn about immunizations, get medical check-ups for children, and obtain assistance from social workers in finding their way onto other elements of the public and private safety net. Finally, it should be noted that men are not eligible for WIC but can apply on behalf of children under the age of five as long as they are legal guardians.

Commodity Supplemental Food Program (CSFP)

A closely related program, also supported by the U.S. Department of Agriculture and administered by the states, is the Commodity Supplemental Food Program, or CSFP, which provides additional quantities of food to low-income pregnant and breastfeeding mothers, mothers up to one year postpartum, children up to the age of six, and those sixty and over. Those sixty and over must fall below 130 percent of FPL, the others below 185 percent, although one cannot be on WIC and CSFP at the same time.[35] Recipients receive packages high in calcium and iron, vitamin A and vitamin C, such as 1 percent milk, skim cheese, infant formula, peanut butter, grits, oats, rice, pasta, canned beef or salmon, and a variety of canned fruits and vegetables.[36]

The Emergency Food Assistance Program (TEFAP)[37]

Another USDA program is TEFAP, or The Emergency Food Assistance Program, which distributes surplus agricultural products to food banks, which in turn pass them on to food pantries, soup kitchens, homeless and domestic violence shelters, and community action agencies, all of which can also pass the food on directly to households as well as serve it in their own facilities.[38] The food allocated to each state is based on the number of poor and unemployed. The USDA also provides funds for the states to administer this program. The food available is quite similar to that provided by CSFP.[39]

National School Breakfast (NSBP) and School Lunch Program (NSLP)

Renewed under the "Healthy, Hunger-Free Kids Act" of 2010, the National School Breakfast and Lunch programs are funded by the Department of Agriculture's Food and Nutrition Service,[40] administered by the respective states, and operated by public and private schools, some public parks that serve large numbers of children, along with other organizations that provide care for poor children (especially during the summer and school breaks) such as Boys & Girls Clubs, and community centers. Any child whose household income falls below 130 percent FPL can get free breakfasts and lunches at participating providers, while children from households under 180 percent FPL pay no more than forty cents per meal. Any child from a household receiving SNAP or Temporary Aid to Families with Dependent Children automatically gets meals for free. It bears noting that the federal government seeks to provide all students with affordable meals, and does so through a mandate that all schools operate their dining services as non-profit programs. On top of this, if a school system served more than 60 percent of its meals to students who received them for free or at the lower rate two years prior (as all five of our cities do), the Department of Agriculture will subsidize that school or other provider.[41] The USDA also provides schools with twenty-two cents' worth of food per meal for each subsidized student.[42] In Kansas City, a secondary school lunch cost $2.30 in 2012, while a subsidized lunch cost only forty cents.[43] In that city's Hickman Mills C-1 school district, the rate of subsidized or free meals is so high, 80 percent, that the state of Missouri deemed it wise to serve the students a free third meal at the end of the school day, just to ensure they are getting the proper nutrition.[44] All Catholic schools in New Orleans that participate in the School Lunch program send children home with applications on the first day of classes in order to get as many enrolled as possible, as hungry children have difficulty concentrating enough to learn. This points to a larger problem regarding the issue of "take-up." One challenge to feeding needy children is that many eligible children do not get free meals because their parents or guardians do not fill out the paperwork. Under the Healthy and Hunger-Free Kids Act of 2010, school systems with very high levels of qualifying students, can serve free meals to all qualifying students if they themselves certify that the child is eligible.[45]

Since 2012, meals served under the NSBP and NSLP programs have been required to meet healthier guidelines. Lunches cannot provide more than 650 calories for fifth graders and below, 700 calories for grades six to eight, and 850 calories for high schoolers, and not more than 10 percent of the calories can come from saturated fat. Sodium levels are also being cut in the 2014/15 school year, and that level will be cut in half over the following ten years.[46] The Secretary of Agriculture also now has the authority to regulate the nutrition standards of foods sold on a school's campus if it is receiving subsidized meals.[47]

To get students to eat breakfast, there are a number of pilot projects being tested in various school districts. In New Orleans, one concern is that many students arrive at school too late to get to the cafeteria before classes begin, so schools there are testing a breakfast in the classroom program where coolers of food are brought to the elementary school classrooms, and students spend the first fifteen minutes or so of the day eating right at their desks. For secondary schools, where students travel from classroom to classroom, New Orleans is experimenting with a Grab 'n Go model of food carts being placed at strategic locations in corridors, so students can grab food and eat in between classes. Another variation of this is providing the food carts during a break in classes after the first class of day. Called "Second Chance Breakfast" in some schools, and Breakfast After First Period, School Brunch or Mid-Morning Nutrition Break in others, this allows students to eat just a little later in the day, perhaps to supplement something they ate earlier, or again, if they arrived to school late. Finally, some high schools are experimenting with breakfast vending machines that provide breakfast foods in machines located throughout the building, but only in the morning hours. As of fall 2013, all breakfasts and lunches served in the Boston public food system will be free to any student, regardless of family income.[48]

California Fruit and Vegetable Program and Special Milk Program

Working under the USDA's Fresh Fruit and Vegetable Program (FFVP), California's Department of Education's Fruit and Vegetable program subsidizes schools, allowing them to be able to offer an additional serving of fruit or vegetables served outside of breakfast or lunch.[49] The Special Milk Program subsidizes the cost of milk, outside of the NSBP and NSLP programs.[50]

Seamless Summer and Child and Adult Care Food Program (CACFP)

In the school system, at least, children are in a controlled environment. On the days they attend, concerned officials can ensure that the children have the opportunity to eat. Ideally, children are being fed breakfast and lunch at school (where they can be provided something healthy), and then parents are using their WIC, SNAP, or CSFP benefits to provide a healthy dinner. But given the low levels of benefits provided, there is always the concern that children will not have enough to eat when school is not in session. To fill this gap, the Food and Nutrition Service's Seamless Summer program allows schools and other providers to offer meals to eligible children even when they are not in session.[51] Likewise, its Child and Adult Care Food Program (CACFP) is similar to the NSBP and NSLP programs, allowing facilities to serve snacks and meals to poor children and certain adults outside of public schools. Quite a wide variety of providers such Head Start programs, non-profit childcare centers, adult daycare facilities, homeless shelters, and even some for-profit providers (if they care for enough qualifying poor) can provide subsidized or free meals, just as school systems can. This program is available for children twelve and under, migrant children fifteen and under, functionally impaired adults or adults sixty and over if they are in daycare facilities, and all children eighteen and under enrolled in after-school programs—again, assuming at least 25 percent of the meals go to recipients who would otherwise get free or reduced cost meals at school.[52] Breakfasts must include milk, fruit or vegetables, and cereals or grains, while lunch and dinners must include milk, meat or an alternative, and at least two different kinds of fruit or vegetables.[53]

As a result of these two programs, eligible children can get free or subsidized meals from a wide range of providers, from schools, whether or not the schools themselves are in session, to childcare facilities, summer programs, and other institutions where they might spend significant amounts of time. A side effect of this is that these programs also allow parents to go to work, since they can be certain their children are being adequately fed even when they are away from home.[54] A child could be fed breakfast and lunch at school, a snack at an after-school program, and then eat a dinner prepared at home that was purchased from funds provided by SNAP and WIC, for example.

Children who grow up malnourished are disproportionately likely to grow up with lasting health and developmental problems, and urban school systems (and the accompanying Boys & Girls Clubs and other food provision networks) often go through quite impressive efforts to provide opportunities for poor children to eat healthy meals, and yet despite those efforts, the programs discussed above are shockingly underutilized. A 2010 study funded by the USDA found that nationwide, just 66 percent of those eligible for SNAP benefits were enrolled in the program.[55] The summer meals program in New Orleans has a mere 13 percent participation rate,[56] leading the school system and non-profits such as the No Kid Hungry[57] to experiment with additional locations and even mobile food trucks,[58] and the USDA is currently running studies in New York to see if adding the funds that would have been sent to dining facilities to recipients' SNAP EBT cards instead increases the likelihood of children eating healthier lunches.

California's Restaurant Meals Program

One theme that we have seen in looking at the nutrition programs listed above is that, while *children* can be fed from school and other non-profit kitchens, for the most part, *adults* are expected to prepare their own meals. WIC even provides cooking classes that teach healthy eating. But of course, for many adults, preparing their own meals can be a true challenge. The homeless lack kitchens and the all the necessary utensils and so forth, while the elderly and disabled may be so infirm that they simply cannot perform many preparation functions. To address this problem, the state of California created the Restaurant Meals program, a subsidiary of CalFresh, in order to "provide a variety of nutritious meal choices to the homeless, disabled, and elderly CalFresh" recipients.[59] Alas, while there are over 1,000 establishments in Los Angeles participating in the Restaurant Meals program, the vast majority are fast food restaurants.[60]

Food Distribution Program on Indian Reservations (FDPIR)[61]

The danger in focusing on urban areas, as this book does, is that we run the risk of ignoring the challenges faced by rural areas, so we would be remiss if we did not discuss America's program to aid Native Americans. One challenge faced by all individuals on SNAP is the ability to get to a store that actually sells items that are both what the household needs and that are also eligible to be purchased under SNAP. In the world of anti-poverty policy, one hears the term "food deserts," referring to locations where there are no food stores within a one-mile radius, although this term is usually employed only to describe urban settings.[62] In urban areas, the problem is often that grocery stores are not located in areas of intense poverty. In rural areas, population density may be so low that grocery stores simply cannot attract enough business to remain open, and for these populations, simply having a SNAP electronic benefit transfer card may be of little use if there is nowhere nearby to use it. Rural Indian reservations often face this difficulty, and in response, the USDA has created an alternative to SNAP that goes under the cumbersome but accurate title of the Food Distribution Program on Indian Reservations (FDPIR). As an alternative to SNAP, participating households have the option of entering FDPIR, in which case they select from a menu of over seventy items and are delivered a package of food once a month. Households can participate in either SNAP or FDPIR, but not both in the same month.[63]

Food Disaster Relief Program[64]

Although not explicitly an anti-poverty program, the Food Disaster Relief Program bears mentioning, especially given the role it played in New Orleans after Hurricane Katrina. As the name implies, this program is aimed at feeding those unable to help themselves due to a natural disaster. Under this program, the USDA's Food and Nutrition Service provides USDA food to states to be distributed through relief shelters and other sites set up after the emergency, including those operated by organizations such as the Red Cross. It also allows agencies to release food directly to households, allowing shelters to focus directly on the displaced. Finally, there is a program called D-SNAP, allowing households that take in the displaced, or that have temporarily seen a decrease in income due to the disaster, to become eligible quickly and somewhat easily.

Food Banks

In the same manner that it is hard to discuss housing without mentioning the role of non-profit shelters, it is likewise hard to discuss nutrition assistance in America's major cities without discussing food banks, which although not governmental organizations, are fundamental to the social safety net. A non-profit subsidiary of Feeding America,[65] the massive Houston Food Bank receives its supplies from a number of sources. In addition to food drives and donations, the food bank works with major supermarket chains, taking in goods that are overstocked, mislabeled, not selling well, or that might go bad. It also collects prepared perishable foods from university dining halls, corporate catering facilities, and area restaurants and hotels, and then distributes over seventy million pounds of food annually to over 500 relief agencies in the greater Houston area from senior and daycare centers to soup kitchens and food pantries. Houston is the largest food bank in the Feeding America system, operating out of a 300,000+-square-foot facility. The Houston Food Bank has also partnered with the Texas Health and Human Services Commission to employ its broad reach to enroll more eligible individuals in SNAP. In another example of public–private partnerships, the food bank's outreach members are now allowed to qualify individuals to enroll into the state's SNAP program directly.[66] Food banks across the nation work with Boys & Girls Clubs to provide after-school meals for children eligible for the School Breakfast and Lunch programs, and often deliver supplemental groceries for monthly distribution to needy households and dairy products to residents of local public housing residences.

With its mission "to feed the hungry people today and work to end hunger tomorrow," Harvesters Community Food Network of Missouri, founded in 1979, plays the same role in Kansas City.[67] Also part of the Feeding America network,[68] Harvesters provides over 15,000 students with healthy snacks each Friday to take home for the weekend as part of its BackSnack program (the idea is that children put the food in their book bags or backpacks),[69] with a similar program for seniors, and delivered over forty million pounds of food in 2011, serving around 66,000 individuals per week.[70]

Summary

Nutrition assistance can be quite valuable for poor children, if their parents or guardians make good use of it. A child can receive a free breakfast and lunch each school day—indeed, even when their school is not even in session—and then go home to a home cooked meal purchased with SNAP and WIC benefits, perhaps supplemented with goods provided from a local food bank or pantry. This is of course contingent on the parents or guardians signing up their children for the proper programs, and again we see the importance of social workers in ensuring this gets done. In the case of nutrition, the key players become members of the school system.

When we examine nutrition assistance targeting adults, the picture changes dramatically. Adults without children discover quickly that there are very few programs aimed at helping them, and what exist often have time limits of just a few months. For these individuals, soup kitchens and food pantries become invaluable.

The fact that nutrition programs are quite comprehensive for children but not for adults without them raises interesting questions. Why are children targeted so heavily? The fact that these programs help America's agricultural interests surely does not hurt, but on the other hand, the nation's powerful construction lobby has not had a similar impact on increasing the amount of public housing being funded by the government, and if interest group politics were at the center of the answer, why are not the far more numerous adults targeted as well? Perhaps instead we should consider that nutrition programs are so heavily centered on children has to do with our understanding of how children are different from adults.

The primary way that children differ, of course, is that they are helpless. Going back to our brief introductory history, children are "the deserving" poor. They are "deserving" of assistance because they are in that position through no fault of their own, while adults have a more difficult time making that argument. In addition, nutrition assistance has another argument, which is that malnourished children are more unlikely to grow into productive workers as adults. As a result, nutrition assistance for children is an area that appeals to individuals across the political spectrum in ways that programs targeting adults simply do not.

Notably, nutrition programs have increasingly come to focus on healthy eating. The fact that SNAP and WIC cards can now be used at many farmers' markets across the country is an extremely new development. While WIC has focused on healthy foods for a very long time, healthier school lunch standards will be less than a year old in 2014, and many cafeterias across the nation will be working to figure out just how to meet them.

We also see in nutrition programs, again, just how closely government programs and non-profits work to protect those in need. Food banks deliver food directly to many public housing projects, for example, while their workers are able to sign up recipients for SNAP benefits in some states. Boys & Girls Clubs across the nation feed children with the same funds that support public cafeterias during the school year.

On the note of public–private partnerships, nutrition assistance leads us to one final comment, and that is on market failure. While not the subject of this book with its tight focus on programs, one fact frequently noted in research is that large numbers of the urban poor live in "food deserts," which are, again, places where there is no access to fresh, healthy, affordable food within a mile radius. The U.S. Department of Agriculture's most recent study indicates that over 23.5 million people live in urban food deserts, and over half of them are poor.[71] Those who own a car may not find this a big deal, but for a single parent working two (or more) jobs, getting to a grocery store without a car can be a challenge, even if there is public transportation. One area that is on the forefront of policy innovation is finding incentives to get stores to open locations in underserved areas, and again in this we see the challenges of policy making in a political community where legislatures are divided by committees, since while this may be seen as an issue of nutrition policy, the solution falls in areas of tax policy, zoning issues, finding insurers willing to provide stores with coverage, and convincing corporate managers that they can operate stores in these areas profitably.

Notes

1 As of 2011, twenty-one states had changed the name to something other than SNAP, mostly to make the program sound more friendly and approachable. http://www.cdph.ca.gov/programs/cpns/Documents/CalFreshOR-%20 Frequently%20Asked%20Questions.pdf (accessed August 2013).

2 http://www.calfresh.ca.gov/ (accessed August 2013).

3 http://www.fns.usda.gov/snap/retailers/eligible.htm (accessed August 2013).

4 http://www.fns.usda.gov/snap/applicant_recipients/facts.htm (accessed August 2013).

5 http://dpss.lacounty.gov/dpss/calfresh/eligibility.cfm (accessed August 2013).

6 http://www.calfresh.ca.gov/PG841.htm (accessed August 2013).

7 http://www.calfresh.ca.gov/PG841.htm#finger (accessed August 2013).

8 http://www.hhsc.state.tx.us/help/Food/snap.shtml (accessed August 2013).

9 http://www.fns.usda.gov/snap/applicant_recipients/eligibility.htm (accessed August 2013).

10 N.B. This may give the impression that millionaires could be on food assistance, but bear in mind that dividends, royalties, rent, and interest still must be counted as income. http://www.calfresh.ca.gov/PG841.htm (accessed August 2013).

11 http://www.dss.state.la.us/index.cfm?md=pagebuilder&tmp=home&pid=93 (accessed August 2013).

12 http://www.fns.usda.gov/snap/government/FY13_Income_Standards.htm. The 200 percent column found at: http://www.familiesusa.org/resources/tools-for-advocates/guides/federal-poverty-guidelines.html (accessed August 2013).

13 http://www.massresources.org/pages.cfm?contentID=12&pageID=3%20& subpages=yes&dynamicID=310 (accessed August 2013).

14 http://www.massresources.org/pages.cfm?contentID=12&pageID=3%20 &subpages=yes&SecondLeveldynamicID=420&DynamicID=418#deductions (accessed August 2013).

15 http://www.massresources.org/heat-eat.html (accessed August 2013).

16 http://www.massresources.org/snap-financial-eligibility.html#SUAs (accessed August 2013).

17 To see how this is calculated, go to http://www.mass.gov/eohhs/docs/dta/g-reg-364.pdf (accessed August 2013).

18 http://www.dss.state.la.us/index.cfm?md=pagebuilder&tmp=home&nid= 34&pnid=7&pid=93&catid=0 (accessed August 2013).

19 http://www.massresources.org/pages.cfm?contentID=12&pageID=3&subpages= yes&dynamicID=789 (accessed August 2013).

20 http://www.beansandgreens.org/ (accessed August 2013).

21 http://www.beansandgreens.org/about/program_highlights.aspx (accessed August 2013).

22 http://www.massresources.org/pages.cfm?contentID=10&pageID=3&subpages= yes&dynamicID=324 (accessed August 2013).

23 http://www.google.com/url?sa=t&rct=j&q=&esrc=s&source=web& cd=1&cad=rja&ved=0CC4QFjAA&url=http%3A%2F%2Fwww.dhh. louisiana.gov%2Fassets%2Foph%2FCenter-PHCH%2FCenter-PH% 2Fnutrition%2Fwic%2FFoodPackageIIIQualifyingandNon-Qualifying Conditions7-09.pdf&ei=FlAeUtWqHpezsATS74GgCQ&usg=AFQj CNGTwy2Z4Z2iVnKBFgijo-KIU-eDPg&sig2=a-JCJetT9arHNuafnqoKeA&bv m=bv.51156542,d.cWc (accessed August 2013).

24 http://www.fns.usda.gov/wic/howtoapply/incomeguidelines.htm (accessed August 2013).

25 http://www.fns.usda.gov/pd/25wifyavgfd$.htm (accessed August 2013).

26 http://www.fns.usda.gov/wic/howtoapply/eligibilityrequirements.htm (accessed August 2013).

27 http://www.nola.gov/RESIDENTS/Health-Department/WIC-Nutrition-Program/ (accessed September 2012).

28 N.B. California's is called the "Golden State Advantage Card." In Texas, it is the "Lone Star Card," and in Louisiana it is called a "Louisiana Purchase Card."

29 For a list on the web, see http://www.mass.gov/eohhs/consumer/basic-needs/ food/wic/participants/wic-food-list.html (accessed August 2013).

30 http://www.mncinc.com/ (accessed August 2013).

31 http://www.mass.gov/agr/massgrown/farmers_markets.htm (accessed August 2013).

32 http://www.fns.usda.gov/wic/benefitsandservices/foodpkgquestions.htm (accessed August 2013).

33 http://www.fns.usda.gov/wic/benefitsandservices/foodpkgquestions.htm (accessed August 2013).

34 For site locations in New Orleans, see http://www.nola.gov/health/programs/wic/ (accessed August 2013).

35 http://www.fns.usda.gov/fdd/programs/csfp/csfp_eligibility.htm (accessed August 2013).

36 For a list, see http://www.fns.usda.gov/fdd/foods/fy12-csfpfoods.pdf (accessed August 2013).

37 http://www.fns.usda.gov/fdd/programs/tefap/ (accessed August 2013).

38 http://www.fns.usda.gov/fdd/programs/tefap/pfs-tefap.pdf. N.B. In Texas, the program is called the Texas Commodity Assistance Program, or TEXCAP.

39 For a list of commodities available for distribution, see http://www.fns.usda.gov/fdd/foods/tefapfoods.pdf (accessed August 2013).

40 http://www.fns.usda.gov/cnd/ (accessed August 2013).

41 http://www.fns.usda.gov/cnd/Lunch/ (accessed August 2013).

42 www.fns.usda.gov/cnd/Lunch/AboutLunch/NSLPFactSheet.pdf (accessed August 2013).

43 http://www.kcpublicschools.org/page/750 (accessed August 2013).

44 http://www.nytimes.com/2011/11/30/education/surge-in-free-school-lunches-reflects-economic-crisis.html (accessed August 2013).

45 http://frac.org/wp-content/uploads/2010/04/cnr_school_nutrition_program_provisions_summary.pdf (accessed August 2013).

46 http://frac.org/highlights-healthy-hunger-free-kids-act-of-2010/. Those interested in Los Angeles might want to read: http://www.latimes.com/health/boostershots/la-heb-school-lunch-makeover-20120125,0,4238045.story (accessed August 2013).

47 http://frac.org/wp-content/uploads/2010/04/cnr_school_nutrition_program_provisions_summary.pdf (accessed August 2013).

48 http://bestpractices.nokidhungry.org/school-breakfast/program-details (accessed August 2013).

49 http://www.cde.ca.gov/ls/nu/sn/caffvp.asp (accessed August 2013).

50 http://www.cde.ca.gov/ls/nu/sn/spm.asp (accessed August 2013).

51 http://www.fns.usda.gov/sfsp/summer-food-service-program-sfsp (accessed August 2013).

52 http://www.fns.usda.gov/cnd/Care/CACFP/aboutcacfp.htm (accessed August 2013).

53 http://www.fns.usda.gov/cnd/care/ (accessed August 2013).

54 For California, see: http://www.cde.ca.gov/ls/nu/sn/ssfofaq.asp (accessed August 2013).

55 Karen E. Cunnyngham and Laura A. Castner, "Reaching Those in Need: State Supplemental Nutrition Assistance Program Participation Rates in 2008." Washington, DC: U.S. Department of Agriculture, Food and Nutrition Service, December 2010. Document No. PP10–152.

56 http://bestpractices.nokidhungry.org/sites/default/files/resources/No%20Kid%20Hungry%20New%20Orleans_Year%20One%20Priorities.pdf (accessed August 2013).

57 http://bestpractices.nokidhungry.org/nkh-campaigns (accessed August 2013).

58 http://bestpractices.nokidhungry.org/summer-meals (accessed August 2013).

59 http://www.ladpss.org/dpss/restaurant_meals/default.cfm (accessed August 2013).

60 http://dpss.co.la.ca.us/dpss/restaurant_meals/pdf/Restaurants_list.pdf (accessed August 2013).

61 http://www.fns.usda.gov/fdd/programs/fdpir/about_fdpir.htm (accessed August 2013).

62 For a map, see http://www.ers.usda.gov/data-products/food-desert-locator/go-to-the-locator.aspx (accessed August 2013).

63 http://hhsa-pg.sdcounty.ca.gov/FoodStamps/63–150/63–166_Food_Distribution_Program_on_Indian_Reservations/63–166_Food_Distribution_Program_on_Indian_Reservations.htm (accessed August 2013).

64 http://www.fns.usda.gov/sites/default/files/Disaster-Relief_Quick_Facts_0.pdf (accessed August 2013).

65 http://feedingamerica.org/default.aspx (accessed August 2013).

66 http://www.houstonfoodbank.org/media/6794/houstonfoodbank_annualreportfy11.pdf (accessed August 2013).

67 http://www.harvesters.org/WhoWeAre/Index.asp?x=020|010&~=(accessed August 2013).

68 http://www.harvesters.org/Link.asp?IdS=0003E7-BCE8A80&Url=http%3A%2F%2Fwww.feedingamerica.org (accessed August 2013).

69 http://www.harvesters.org/WhoWeAre/Index.asp?Reference=BackSnack&~= (accessed August 2013).

70 http://www.harvesters.org/WhoWeAre/Index.asp?x=020|010&~=(accessed August 2013).

71 http://apps.ams.usda.gov/fooddeserts/foodDeserts.aspx (accessed August 2013).

Chapter 5

Medical Assistance

Our final area of focus is providing the poor and needy either with healthcare directly, or more often, with health insurance so they can obtain healthcare on the private market. The American healthcare system changed dramatically on January 1, 2014, with the implementation of health insurance marketplaces, created by the Affordable Care Act of 2010. Prior to the ACA, there were Americans who could not obtain health insurance, either because they could not afford it, or because they had a pre-existing health condition that rendered them uninsurable. Policy research will now be shifting from the uninsured to those who are newly insured, and we are entering a period in American history that is unusually rich for healthcare researchers.

Affordable Care Act

On March 23, 2010, President Barack Obama signed the Patient Protection and Affordable Care Act (PPACA) into law, typically referred as either the "ACA" or "Obamacare." Among other things, the law mandates that in 2014, all Americans must be enrolled in a health insurance plan, and that each state must offer its residents affordable health insurance plans that can be purchased individually or as a family through a marketplace. The idea is that in each state, either the state government or the federal government will have negotiated with private health insurance companies to offer plans on the given state's health insurance marketplace that offer health insurance with certain cost-sharing features, at a given price. All plans will cover the same ten Essential Health Benefits, that include, among others, preventative care (which will be free), inpatient and outpatient services, prescription drugs, maternity and newborn care, laboratory services, habilitative and rehabilitative services, and mental health and substance abuse treatments.[1] Households will have the choice of selecting plans on the basis of "metal levels," which offer the same benefits, but at different premium levels, which will determine how much of the costs are borne by the purchaser, and how much by the insurer. At the lowest level, the bronze plans offer the least expensive premiums, but the insurers will pick up, on average, only around 60 percent of the costs. Note that this does not mean that the insurer will cover 60 percent of the costs for every individual, since some people will have virtually no costs whatsoever while others will run expenses up to the Out-of-Pocket Maximum ($6,350 for an individual and $12,700 for a family), but rather for the entire pool of people in the plan, the insurer will cover roughly 60 percent of the costs. In return for the most expensive premiums, the platinum plans will cover roughly 90 percent of the costs.

Each state will have a health insurance marketplace, sometimes called "exchanges," which will either be administered entirely by the state (State-Based Exchanges), such as Massachusetts and California, jointly operated marketplaces where states may, for example, do the marketing and work with the private carriers (Federal Partnership Exchanges), and states where the federal government runs the entire marketplace in all of its aspects (Federally Facilitated Exchanges), which is what Texas, Louisiana, and Kansas are doing. Regardless of the model, the experience for the consumer purchasing insurance in a marketplace will be quite similar, as will be the offerings.

In some states, households will have many plans from which to choose, while in smaller states, there may just be two or three insurers—although that is likely the case on the private market in those states as well. In any event, the government is not taking over the health insurance industry, but instead following the classic route of public–private cooperation, where, in exchange for offering affordable plans at perhaps higher levels of regulation, health insurance companies in return will have access to millions and millions of new customers—anywhere from seven to twenty-two million over the next few years—who otherwise would have remained uninsured, having incomes too high for Medicaid (to be discussed below), but too low to be able to afford insurance on their own.

The Affordable Care Act gave states the option of allowing households with incomes up to 133 percent FPL to enter the Medicare system. Previously, the limit was 100 percent FPL. In any event, the federal government has created a system of subsidies for households falling under 400 percent FPL, both to help them pay for the premiums and also offset the expenses of co-pays and deductibles. Households under 400 percent are eligible to receive Premium Tax Credits, which are deductions to the income taxes that help offset the costs of paying the health insurance premiums on the marketplace. Households can take the tax credit when they file their taxes, or they can take them monthly and in advance, known as Advanced Premium Tax Credit (APTC). Using APTC, the individual or family will see their monthly premiums reduced, with the federal government paying the difference. Households may also be able to receive cost-sharing, in which the federal government (supplemented by states in many cases) will have a portion of their deductibles and co-pays paid for them.[2]

The Health Insurance Marketplaces went into effect on January 1, 2014, and as of when this book went to print, were still very much works in progress. But one state, Massachusetts, has had its marketplace up and running for several years and has served as a model for PPACA. We can look at the many programs offered by Massachusetts to see what has until now essentially been the most generous and comprehensive system of public health provision in the nation.

Health Insurance Programs in Massachusetts

Massachusetts Governor Mitt Romney signed the landmark Massachusetts Health Reform Act into law in June of 2006. It required that every resident of the state be covered by health insurance or pay a state income tax penalty. One element of the law was to provide incentives for all employers of more than ten employees to provide coverage by mandating that they either offer healthcare plans to their employees with a "fair and reasonable" contribution toward the costs, or help subsidize public insurance options by paying up to $295 a year per employee. The law also mandated that every adult have health insurance or be fined up to half the annual costs of the least expensive insurance plan offered under Commonwealth Choice (discussed below). Given that it mandates all adults have health insurance, the Commonwealth of Massachusetts has worked to develop a wide array of plans to ensure that all who need health insurance can find a manner to procure it, and there is a wide array of programs available to the needy.[3]

The federal government solely funds Medicare, a program for those over age sixty-five, along with individuals who are permanently disabled or who have end-stage renal disease or ALS. Medicaid is a joint federal-state program for the poor in which each state develops its own set of programs that can vary to a certain extent as long as they meet certain minimum requirements. A second joint program targeting children is the Children's Health Insurance Program (CHIP), created by Congress to ensure that every child is covered by health insurance. In Massachusetts, Medicaid and CHIP have been integrated into a set of programs that go under the name MassHealth. Additionally, there is a federal health insurance program for active-duty and retired military personnel and their families (TRICARE) and another state insurance program for those involved in the maritime trades (Fishing Partnership Health Plan), since fishing has in the past been considered so dangerous that those involved in it had great difficulty finding a company willing to insure them. Massachusetts also created a set of programs to help those who either cannot afford health insurance or who cannot obtain coverage due to existing conditions, but who do not qualify for Medicare or Medicaid. These are the Commonwealth Care programs, under which health insurance is provided by commercial providers who have designed programs specifically for recipients that are affordable yet still provide a minimum basket of coverage. Finally, there are a number of boutique programs dedicated to filling the holes in the safety net for those who are in need but do not qualify for the broader programs.

To get started in obtaining public health insurance, residents begin by filling out a Medical Benefits Request (MBR), which is a common application for all programs administered by Massachusetts.[4] This allows program officers to place applicants accurately, since as we shall see, there are many programs and finding the right one is quite complicated.

Insurance Partnership

A central public policy goal for Governor Mitt Romney and the Massachusetts state legislators was to facilitate employers covering as many of the state's residents as possible. To help small businesses employing fewer than fifty employees, the state created a program known as the Insurance Partnership.[5] Businesses must agree to pay at least 50 percent of the premiums for a plan that provides comprehensive coverage, and must initially have at least one uninsured employee. Employees can qualify if they are between nineteen and sixty-four years of age, have not been offered health insurance by their employers in the past six months and do not have a spouse who is eligible, and have a gross family income that falls under the guidelines listed in Table 5.1.

The Insurance Partnership will help pay the employee's premiums, and will also subsidize the employer up to $1,000 per year for its share of the costs, making covering a formerly uninsured employee more affordable for both parties.

MassHealth

MassHealth is the Massachusetts version of two programs that are jointly funded by the federal government and the states, aiming to provide health insurance to the poor, especially poor children. The first program is Medicaid, a medical program created in 1965 as part of the Johnson administration's Great Society platform of helping the nation's poorest obtain healthcare. The second program is the Children's Health Insurance Program (CHIP), created in 1997 to help families with children find coverage when their incomes are slightly higher than what they need to qualify for Medicaid.[6] In short, MassHealth "aims to help children, adults working for small employers, pregnant women, disabled individuals, unemployed

Table 5.1 Maximum Annual Gross Family Income by Family Size to Qualify for the Insurance Partnership[7]

Family Size	Maximum Annual Gross Family Income
1	$34,476
2	$46,536
3	$58,596
4	$70,656
5	$82,716

individuals, parents and caretakers of children, HIV positive individuals, people requiring long-term care, Department of Mental Health clients, and women with breast or cervical cancer, and elderly people."[8] The federal government's 2010 Health Insurance Reform Act mandates that no state can cut benefits or tighten eligibility requirements of either Medicaid or CHIP for the next several years, although it does allow states to expand them in order to allow more households into the programs. All recipients of Transitional Aid to Families with Dependent Children automatically qualify for MassHealth.

Administered by the Massachusetts Executive Office of Health and Human Services, MassHealth assists needy individuals obtain health coverage in one of two ways. Firstly, MassHealth can help low-earners who are eligible to purchase health insurance through their employers by paying the premiums for them. The second method is by providing health plans directly to recipients.

There are seven MassHealth programs, and the differences between them can appear daunting because the programs are meant to serve different constituents, but there is a certain order to the programs, with most having one program to serve the absolute poorest, and then a second version to serve the same sets of population that earn slightly more.

MassHealth Standard[9]

MassHealth Standard is the most generous program offered, covering a wide array of inpatient and outpatient services, medical services (such as lab tests, hearing aids and eyeglasses, and pharmacy needs), and mental health and substance abuse care. The full list can be seen in Table 5.2. As mentioned above, Standard can also help pay for a commercial health insurance plan, either through an employer or purchased via some other route. One issue about qualifying for Standard is that *each individual in the family must qualify separately,* and there are different income demands depending on one's age, such that an infant or child may qualify for the Standard program while the parents may not. To qualify for Standard, pregnant women must have an income less than 200 percent of the Federal Poverty Line, infants under one year old qualify if their household also has an income less than 200 percent FPL, but children one to eighteen only qualify if the households fall under the more stringent 150 percent FPL, and parents and disabled adults 133 percent FPL.

Importantly, because all families on TAFDC are automatically eligible for MassHealth, the program must be designed in a manner that encourages recipients to find employment. One way MassHealth does this is by allowing those on it to remain covered for up to one full year in the same program if they would otherwise be ineligible because of their new income limits after returning to work. Whether true or not, there were at least stories of

Table 5.2 Program Characteristics for MassHealth Standard[10]

Covered Services (There May be Some Limits)	Eligibility Characteristics	Maximum Income Standards
• Inpatient hospital services • Outpatient services: hospitals, clinics, doctors, dentists, family planning, and vision care • Medical services: lab tests, x-rays, therapies, pharmacy services,* eyeglasses, hearing aids, medical equipment and supplies, adult day health, and adult foster care • Behavioral health (mental health and substance abuse) services • Well-child screenings (for children under the age of 21) including: medical, vision, dental, hearing, behavioral health (mental health and substance abuse), and developmental screens, as well as shots • Long-term-care services at home or in a long-term-care facility, including home-health services • Transportation services • Quit-smoking services	• Pregnant • Under age 19 • A parent living with children under age 19* • Disabled according to the standards set by federal law; or • One was eligible and is within 12 months of losing that status* *These benefits are also available for parents and caretaker relatives who are aged 65 or older	• For pregnant women: 200% of the federal poverty level • For children under age 1: 200% of the federal poverty level • For children aged 1 through 18: 150% of the federal poverty level • For parents or caretaker relatives of children under age 19: 133% of the federal poverty level • For disabled adults: 133% of the federal poverty level

*If the applicants are eligible for both Medicare and MassHealth, Medicare will provide most of the prescription drug coverage through a Medicare prescription drug plan Note: For disabled adults who also get Medicare Part B, MassHealth will pay the Medicare premium, and if applicable, the coinsurance and deductibles

recipients not wanting to accept job offers out of fear of losing their Medicaid coverage.

MassHealth CommonHealth[11]

MassHealth CommonHealth offers almost the exact same set of benefits as Standard does (including paying for premiums for commercially provided health plans), but is a dedicated program for the disabled. Any child or adult classified as disabled under state and federal law can qualify for Common-Health as long as adults work no more than forty hours per month, and those who have incomes above 100 percent FPL may have to cost share, paying graduated percentages of premiums and co-pays.

MassHealth Family Assistance[12]

MassHealth Family Assistance, normally referred to simply as Family, is different from Standard and CommonHealth in that it does not offer its own health plan. Family is primarily for working families with incomes too high to qualify for Standard or CommonHealth but who can get insurance through their employer and need help with the premiums. It also helps them obtain certain services not offered by their employer's plan. If obtaining insurance through work is not possible, Family will help the family enroll in a Primary Care Clinician (PCC) Plan.

As the name implies, Family is for households with children under the age of nineteen in them, although it is also open to handicapped individuals and people who are HIV positive. Someone in the household must work for an employer that is part of the Insurance Partnership, and be eligible to purchase into a plan that offers benefits equal to or higher than those of MassHealth Standard. Household members must also have high enough earnings not to qualify for Standard or CommonHealth (otherwise they would default into one of those instead), and yet not earn above 200 percent FPL if an adult or 300 percent for most children.

MassHealth Basic[13]

The Basic program is specially designed for individuals receiving services from the State Department of Mental Health. Its services are essentially the same as those offered by Standard. One must neither be working nor have worked enough to be eligible for Unemployment Insurance over the past year, and fall under 100 percent FPL.

MassHealth Essential[14]

Medicaid is not open to illegal immigrants, yet of course, these individuals, like all human beings, will sooner or later find themselves in need of medical care. To grapple with this reality, and also with the fact that the state mandates all adults to have health coverage, Massachusetts has set up two programs for illegal immigrants. Funded without federal dollars, MassHealth Essential offers the same coverage as Standard does, only for immigrants who do not qualify for it due to their immigration status. Just as with Common-Health and Basic, Essential is open to any eligible recipient whose household income falls below 100 percent FPL.

To summarize so far, MassHealth Standard bears that name because it is, in effect, the gold standard of Medicaid policies in Massachusetts. Common-Health, Basic, and Essential are effectively the same programs, only for the specialized communities of the disabled, those with mental health issues, and illegal immigrants, respectively. Culling out those categories of recipients allows the state to have dedicated staff to serve those individuals with a deep understanding of their particular needs.

MassHealth Limited[15]

The least attractive of the programs listed so far, MassHealth Limited is for illegal immigrants whose household earnings are too high for them to qualify for Essential. As with Standard, pregnant women will be covered if their household income falls below 200 percent PFL, along with infants under one year of age. Children aged one to eighteen will qualify if their household's income is below 150 percent FPL, while parents and disabled adults need to have incomes below 133 percent FPL. MassHealth Limited covers medical emergencies and little more, paying for ambulance and emergency room services, inpatient and outpatient care associated with a medical emergency, and labor and child delivery, along with pharmacy services also associated with an emergency.

MassHealth Prenatal[16]

The final MassHealth program is specifically for pregnant women. Any pregnant woman can be enrolled in MassHealth Prenatal almost immediately, and will be covered for two months, during which time she can receive routine prenatal office visits and care. If her income is over 200 percent FPL, there will be some cost-sharing. During that time, the individual must apply for MassHealth, and at the end of the sixty-day period, the expectation is that the individual will have been placed in an appropriate program. The moving force behind Prenatal is ensuring the birth of a healthy child, allowing the mother to receive any medical treatment—and indeed get the necessary check-ups to learn if she even needs treatment. If we note from above that all pregnant women and all infants under the age of one qualify for MassHealth Standard if their incomes are below 200 percent FPL, we can see how Prenatal can serve as a stopgap measure while the applicant's paperwork makes its way through the system.

Commonwealth Choice and Commonwealth Care

The passage of the Massachusetts Health Reform Act of 2006 made it mandatory for every adult in the state to enroll in a healthcare plan, raising the obvious dilemma of what happens to individuals and families who earned too high an income to qualify for MassHealth and not enough to afford one of the traditional commercially-offered plans. Proponents of the bill gathered various stakeholders, including employers, unions, groups tasked to represent the poor, academics, and importantly, health insurance companies, and created a new independent state agency called the Health Connector, whose role was and remains to determine the minimum coverage for an eligible Commonwealth Choice plan and to negotiate with health insurers the premiums participants will be charged for them.

The Connector also partners with industry groups such as the "Associated Industries of Massachusetts, the Retailers Association of Massachusetts, the Massachusetts Chapter of the National Federation of Independent Business and many local chambers of commerce" to help educate eligible individuals about their options.[17]

Commonwealth Care

Commonwealth Care is open to any Massachusetts adult resident or legal alien who earns below 300 percent of the Federal Poverty Line, listed in Table 5.3 (children will be covered by MassHealth). Participants are given the choice of enrolling in one of five different health plans, all of which offer the same menu of medical services, including a primary care physician, preventative check-ups, inpatient and outpatient care, prescription drug coverage, vision care, and treatment for drug and alcohol abuse and mental health problems. Some plans also offer dental coverage.

Care programs offer three tiers of coverage, Plan Types 1, 2, and 3, each with different levels of co-payments and benefits based on the recipient's income (see Table 5.4). Plan Type 1 is open to households that fall below 100 percent FPL, and will have small co-payments but no premiums or deductibles. Plan Type 2 is open to households that fall between 100 percent

Table 5.3 Maximum Annual Family Incomes for Commonwealth Care Eligibility[18]

Household Size	Maximum Annual Income	Maximum Monthly Income
1	$ 33,516	$2,793
2	$ 45,396	$3,783
3	$ 57,276	$4,773
4	$ 69,156	$5,763
5	$ 81,036	$6,753
6	$ 92,916	$7,743
7	$104,796	$8,733
8	$116,676	$9,723

Table 5.4 Co-Payment Costs per Commonwealth Care Plan Type[19]

Plan Type	Monthly Premiums	Inpatient Services Co-Pay (Per Stay)	Doctor's Office Co-Pay	Emergency Care Co-Pay	Prescription Drug Co-Pay (Generic)	Maximum Annual Co-Pay for Prescriptions
1	None	None	None	None	$ 1 or $3.65	$200
2	$ 0–$28*	$ 50	$10	$ 50	$10	$400
3	$40–$81**	$250	$15	$100	$12.50	$650

*This is the range of premiums from lowest to highest for a household at 200% FPL
**This is the range of premiums from lowest to highest for a household at 300% FPL

and 200 percent FPL, although only households that earn over 150 percent FPL will pay a premium. Plan Type 3 is open to households that fall between 200 percent and 300 percent FPL.

Commonwealth Choice

The Health Connector has given its Seal of Approval to a number of plans created by companies such as Blue Cross Blue Shield of Massachusetts, Fallon Community Health Care, Harvard Pilgrim Health Care, Health New England, Neighborhood Health Plan, and Tufts Health Plan to cover individuals in need of health insurance but earning too much to qualify for MassHealth or Commonwealth Care. Not all plans cover the entire state, but all offer services in Boston. Within each plan, insurers offer three payment varieties, called the Bronze, Silver, and Gold options. Bronze options have lower monthly premiums, but higher co-pays and deductibles. As the plans move to Silver and then Gold, the monthly premiums rise, but the co-pays and deductibles fall. Within each category, there are then low, medium, and high benefit packages, allowing one to choose from a Bronze low benefit package at one end to a Gold high benefit package at the other (see Table 5.5).

Children's Medical Security Plan (CMSP)

Children who are not eligible for MassHealth and whose parents cannot afford Commonwealth Care can still be covered under a very barebones program known as the Children's Medical Security Plan (CMSP), which is operated by MassHealth, with claim processing, customer service, and premium collection being performed by a private contractor.[20]

Services covered by CMSP include:

- routine check-ups
- immunizations

Table 5.5 Sample Commonwealth Choice Plans and Benefits: Massachusetts Blue Cross Blue Shield Plans, Family with One Adult and Two Children[21]

Plan	Monthly Premium	Annual Deductible	Maximum Annual Out-of-Pocket Expenses	Co-pay for a Doctor's Visit	Generic Prescriptions	Emergency Room	Hospital Stay
Bronze Low	$ 751.06	$2,000 (ind) $4,000 (fam)	$ 5,000 (ind) $10,000 (fam)	$25	$15 co-pay	Annual deductible, then $100 co-pay	Annual deductible, then 20% of coinsurance
Silver High	$1,147.29	None	$ 2,000 (ind) $ 4,000 (fam)	$25	$15 co-pay	$100 co-pay	Annual deductible, then no co-pay
Gold	$1,473.93	None	None	$20	$15 co-pay	$ 75 co-pay	$150 co-pay

- office visits when child is sick or hurt
- lab tests, x-rays, and other diagnostic tests
- outpatient surgery for tympanostomy ear tubes or for inguinal hernia
- family planning services
- prescription medicines (up to $200 per child per year)
- rental or purchase of prescribed medical equipment (up to $200 per child per year; up to $500 per child per year for asthma, diabetes, or epilepsy)
- eye exams and hearing tests
- outpatient mental health and substance abuse visits (up to twenty visits per year)
- dental coverage includes the following services, up to $750 per child per year:
  - exams and cleanings (twice per year)
  - x-rays
  - fluoride treatment (twice per year)
  - sealants (once per year)
  - fillings, extractions, and root canals
  - crowns
  - space maintainers.

Children enrolled in CMSP may also enroll simultaneously in the Health Safety Net (see next section), which may help with covering some of these services.

To determine what expenses a household would pay under Children's Medical Security Plan, one would start by determining whether the gross household income falls under 200 percent, 300 percent, or 400 percent FPL.

A family, or more likely a program officer, would take the household's gross monthly income, find what category they are in according to Table 5.6, and then apply it to Table 5.7 to see how much they would pay for various services.

As one can see, premiums and co-pays are at points half or lower what they would be under the Commonwealth Care and Choice plans, although of course, the coverage provided is significantly smaller as well, and if a child required ambulance or hospitalization services, CMSP would not assist with payments. Thus, this program must be used in conjunction with the Health Safety Net.

Health Safety Net

The Health Safety Net is the final fallback for adults who are not eligible for MassHealth and either cannot afford or are unwilling to pay into one of the Commonwealth Care or Choice systems. This program can also be used with the Children's Medical Security Plan to cover children under the

Table 5.6 Gross Household Monthly Income Limits for CMSP, by Family Size[22]

Family Size	200% of FPL	300% of FPL	400% of FPL
1	$1,915	$2,873	$ 3,830
2	$2,585	$3,888	$ 5,170
3	$3,255	$4,883	$ 6,510
4	$3,925	$5,888	$ 7,850
5	$4,595	$6,893	$ 9,190
6	$5,265	$7,898	$10,530
7	$5,935	$8,903	$11,870
8	$6,605	$9,908	$13,210
Each extra person	+$ 670	+$1,005	+$ 1,340

Table 5.7 CMSP Expenses by Income for Various Family Sizes[23]

Annual Household Income Before Taxes	Monthly Premium	Co-pay Medical	Co-pay Dental	Co-pay Pharmacy
< 200% FPL	No charge	$2	$2	
200%–300% FPL	$7.80 per child per month with a maximum of $23.40 per family per month	$5	$4	$3 per generic drug $4 per brand-name drug
301%–400% FPL	$33.14 per family per month	$5	$4	
>400% FPL	$38.99 per child per month	$8	$6	

age of nineteen. Operated by the Massachusetts Division of Health Care Finance and Policy, the Health Safety Net replaced the Uncompensated Care Pool, known as "Free Care" in October of 2007, with the goal of ensuring that any resident of Massachusetts without regard to income, immigration status, or medical condition can receive medically necessary treatments when needed. It is structured to allow someone to walk into a hospital or community health center and as long as they have proof of identification, Massachusetts residence and income, they can apply for the program and receive services on the spot. Moreover, the program will also pay for any covered services received six months prior to application as well.[24] These services include:

- medical visits
- lab, diagnostic testing, and radiology services
- obstetrics and family planning
- surgical procedures
- audiology
- podiatry
- pharmacy services
- behavioral health
- diabetes self-management
- tobacco cessation services
- dental services
- vision care
- medical nutrition therapy.

These services can only be delivered at a community health center. Some inpatient services will also be covered at hospitals.

To determine eligibility, the applicants once again must turn first to Table 5.6 to determine into which category they fall, and then examine Table 5.8.

Adults in households that fall above 200 percent FPL will have to pay an annual deductible, according to the following formula:

Annual deductible = [(Gross family income) − (200 percent FPL)] * 40%

We can use the example of a family of three with an annual income of $40,000. Looking at Table 5.6, they fall above the 200 percent FPL of (12 * $3,255 =) $39,060.

$40,000 − $39,060 = $940, which would be multiplied by .40 to determine the annual deductible. $940 * .40 = $376. So the annual deductible would be $376 for this household.

Medical Security Plan

Massachusetts is the only state in the nation to have a healthcare plan exclusively for individuals receiving Unemployment Insurance. The Medical Security Plan (MSP) offers two types of benefits. For those eligible for COBRA,[25] a federal law administered by the Department of Labor allowing workers who have left their employment to continue receiving healthcare coverage from their existing plan, MSP's Premium Assistance plan may pay up to 80 percent of the costs for those who must pay 100 percent of their COBRA premiums without subsidy from their former employer. MSP also offers a Health Maintenance Organization (HMO) plan through Blue Cross Blue Shield of Massachusetts.

Table 5.8 Costs for Health Safety Net Service, by Income Level[26]

Services	Children age 18 and under	Adults with Family Income 0%–100% FPL	Adults with Family Income 101%–200% FPL	Adults with Family Income 201%–400% FPL
Prescription drugs (Generic/ Preferred)	$0 / $0	$1* or $3.65	$1* or $3.65	$1* or $3.65
Community health center services	$0	$ 0	$ 0	Percentage of the bill until recipient has paid the annual deductible
Emergency room visit	$0	$ 0	$ 0	
Outpatient hospital visit	$0	$ 0	$ 0	
Inpatient hospital admission	$0	$ 0	$ 0	$250
Maximum annual pharmacy co-payments	$0	$250	$250	$250
Annual deductible	None	None	None	40% of the difference between family income and 200% FPL

* Generic antihypertensives for high blood pressure, antihyperlipidemics for high cholesterol, and antihyperglycemics for diabetes cost $1. Other generics cost $2

Medicare

Medicare is a federal program created in 1965 as part of President Lyndon Baines Johnson's Great Society platform. Originally designed to give seniors access to medical care, the program was expanded in 1972 to include the permanently disabled, those with end-stage renal disease (requiring kidney dialysis), and those who have Amyotrophic Lateral Sclerosis (ALS, or "Lou Gehrig's disease"). Medicare is open to all qualified individuals, without regard to means testing, and forms a key pillar of the American social safety net, covering roughly one-tenth of the American population. Medicare has four parts to it, labeled simply Part A, Part B, Part C, and Part D.

Part A provides insurance for hospital stays, also known as inpatient services, along with stays at nursing homes or skilled nursing facilities—if the stay is related to a diagnosis stemming from a hospital stay, but not otherwise—a hospice stay, treatment provided by home-health agencies, and blood transfusions.[27] As long as one has worked and contributed to Social Security for forty quarters during one's life, then there are no premiums for this coverage, although recipients have, of course, paid a 1.45 percent payroll tax while working, as did their employers.[28] Those who do have to pay a premium will pay up to $441 per month in 2013.[29] Anyone who is eligible to receive Social Security is automatically eligible for Part A. Part A recipients still do have to pay a deductible, though. For inpatient stays, the individual will pay for the first $1,156 of costs out of their own pocket, and if their hospital stay lasts longer than two months, they will have to pay $289 per day for days 61 through 90, and $578 per day for days 91 to 150. If they are staying in a skilled nursing facility, they will pay a co-pay of $144.50 per day for days 21 through 100.[30] After that, the patient pays the full costs of the remaining stay.

Part B provides insurance coverage for doctor's visits and outpatient services. Roughly 75 percent of the expenses are covered by general revenues from the federal government, with monthly premiums paid by the elderly filling the remainder of the expenses. For 2012, monthly premiums were set at $99.90, although roughly three-quarters of the insured will still pay the 2009 premium of $96.40.[31] The 2013 premium structure can be seen in Table 5.9.

Part B also has a $147 annual deductible, and once over that, the participant pays 20 percent of any further costs under the plan.[32]

Part C, previously called "Medicare+Choice" and now known as Medicare Advantage, offers the services of Parts A and B through Health Maintenance Organizations (HMOs). The HMOs are required to offer the same coverage as Parts A and B, but not necessarily at the same price levels (since, for the moment, providers get reimbursed at higher rates than Parts A and B do),[33] and they have the option of either offering additional coverage, or they can charge additional premiums for extra services, such as dental or eye, for example. These plans can also negotiate with nursing homes or hospitals for lower fees, which they can also either pass on to consumers or use to offer extra coverage. Medicare Advantage plans also offer Part D prescription drug coverage.

Part D was created as part of the Medicare Prescription Drug, Improvement, and Modernization Act of 2003 under President George W. Bush and went into effect in 2006. It provides prescription drug coverage to everyone receiving Medicare, either through their Medicare Advantage HMO or through a Prescription Drug Plan (PDP). Benefits will vary from plan to

Table 5.9 Total Medicare Part B Premiums by Income for 2013[34]

Beneficiaries who File a 2011 Individual Tax Return with Income	Beneficiaries who File a 2011 Joint Tax Return with Income	Total Monthly Premium Amount
≤$85,000	≤$170,000	$104.90
$85,000.01 to $107,000	$170,000.01 to $214,000	$146.90
$107,000.01 to $160,000	$214,000.01 to $320,000	$209.80
$160,000.01 to $214,000	$320,000.01 to $428,000	$272.70
≥$214,000	≥$428,000	$335.70

plan, allowing seniors to choose a plan that offers the best benefits for their needs. Premiums also vary dramatically. To assist participants with selecting a plan, Medicare created a website entitled the Prescription Drug Plan Finder.[35]

Part D has a payment system that can be daunting to understand. The key to understanding payments is that as the individual pays more and more through the course of the calendar year, they and the federal government will pay different percentages of the costs. At the start of the year, the individual pays out the first $325 out of his or her own pocket for prescription drugs annually. After that, for the next $2,645 in expenses, Medicare will pay 75 percent of costs (up to the point where there are $2,970 in expenses), with the individual paying the other 25 percent out-of-pocket. Once the $2,970 threshold has been reached, individuals are on their own in what is commonly called the "donut hole," until total out-of-pocket expenses have reached $4,750 in costs (although 50 percent of the costs of brand-name drugs will be paid for by the manufacturer even though it will still "count" as though the individual spent 100 percent for purposes of getting out of the donut hole).[36] After that the plan's catastrophic coverage kicks in, with Medicare picking up 95 percent of the costs for the remainder of the year. The donut hole is gradually being closed due to the Affordable Care Act, and will no longer exist in the year 2020. Medicare participants have an enormous array of commercial plans open to them.[37]

Extra Help

Households with limited means can apply for a program called Medicare Extra Help. To qualify for assistance (at any level), one cannot have assets over $13,300 for an individual or $26,580 for a married couple (not counting car or house or $1,500 per person for burial), and annual income over $17,235 for an individual or $23,265 for a couple.[38] The benefits available per income and asset level are found in Table 5.10, and are used in conjunction with Medicare Part D.

Prescription Advantage[39]

Operated by the Commonwealth of Massachusetts Executive Office of Elder Affairs, Prescription Advantage is a prescription drug insurance plan available to all residents over the age of sixty-five, as well as younger residents with disabilities, as long as they meet the same income and asset requirements listed for Medicare Extra Help above and meet work requirements. This plan is designed to work with Medicare and Medicare Extra Help, although it also has plans for individuals not on Medicare.

Prescription Advantage requires anyone applying who is eligible for Medicare to enroll in it. Medicare serves as the primary insurer, and Prescription

Table 5.10 Medicare's "Extra Help" Plan, 2013[40]

Plan	Annual Income and Asset Limits	Deductible and Premiums	Co-Pays	Help for Catastrophic Costs
Level 1	$11,490 in income for an individual or $15,510 for a couple $8,580 for an individual or $13,620 for a couple	Premium: None Deductible: None	$1.15 co-pay for generic drugs on the plan's drug list $3.50 co-pay for brand-name drugs on the plan's drug list	If one's total drug costs go over $6,733.75 for the year, the individual will have no co-pay for drugs on the plan's drug list
Level 2	$15,512 for an individual or $20,939 for a couple $8,580 for an individual or $13,620 for a couple	Premium: None Deductible: None	$2.65 co-pay for generic drugs on the plan's drug list $6.60 co-pay for brand-name drugs on the plan's drug list	If one's total drug costs go over $6,733.75 for the year, the individual will have no co-pay for drugs on the plan's drug list
Level 3	$17,235 for an individual or $23,265 for a couple $13,300 for an individual or $26,580 for a couple	Premium: Sliding Scale Deductible: $66	15% up to $6,733.75	If one's total drug costs go over $6,733.75 for the year, one pays: $2.65 co-pay generic drugs on the plan's drug list $6.60 co-pay for brand-name drugs on the plan's drug list

Advantage works as the secondary insurer, filling in the gaps of Part D at various points for individuals of different income and asset levels. For some it will pay co-payments, cover the "donut hole," and lower the roof on catastrophic payments before Medicare again kicks in. Benefits can be seen in Table 5.11.

Prescription Advantage also helps with drugs not covered by Medicare. It will pay the full costs of a one-time prescription for seventy-two hours of any medication that cannot be billed to Medicare.

The program may also help individuals with co-payments if they are in health plans other than Medicare, if those plans offer better coverage, but the likelihood of individuals both being in a better plan and falling under the income eligibility is not high. Prescription Advantage will also help eligible individuals who require prescription drug coverage but who are not eligible for Medicare. "This coverage has no monthly premium. Depending on income, members will pay a co-payment for prescription drugs and will have an annual out-of-pocket spending limit and quarterly deductible. Once

Table 5.11 Prescription Advantage Benefit Plans[41]

Category	Income Limits (Individual/ Couple)	Premium Assistance?	Deductible	Co-Pay	Out-of-Pocket Limit
S0	$15,512 individual $20,939 couple	Prescription Advantage does not pay any portion of drug plan premiums. Extra Help may cover all or part of the premium costs	No deductibles and no payments during the "donut hole" phase	$2.65 or $6.60 per prescription	Members in this category do not pay deductibles. The only out-of-pocket expenses are co-pays
S1	$17,235 individual $23,265 couple	Prescription Advantage does not pay any portion of drug plan premiums. Extra Help may cover all or part of the premium costs	If the member's Medicare drug plan co-payments are higher, then they will pay no more than the Prescription Advantage co-payment limits of $7 for generic drugs or $18 for brand-name drugs for a 30-day supply, and Prescription Advantage will pay the difference	$7 for generic drugs or $18 for brand-name drugs for a 30-day supply. This co-pay structure will continue until the member's out-of-pocket limit is reached	Members will pay no more than $1,510 in out-of-pocket expenses in the calendar year
S2	$21,601 individual $29,159 couple*	No	When a member reaches the limit to trigger the "donut hole" at $2,970, Prescription Advantage will begin covering any difference between the individual's co-pay under the Medicare plan and the co-pays listed in the next column	$7 for generic drugs or $18 for brand-name drugs for a 30-day supply once deductible limit has been reached. This co-pay structure will continue until the member's out-of-pocket limit is reached	Members will pay no more than $1,675 in out-of-pocket expenses in the calendar year

S3	$25,835 individual $34,898 couple **	No	When a member reaches the limit to trigger the "donut hole" at $2,970, Prescription Advantage will begin covering any difference between the individual's co-pay under the Medicare plan and the co-pays listed in the next column	$12 for generic drugs or $30 for brand-name drugs for a 30-day supply once deductible limit has been reached. This co-pay structure will continue until the member's out-of-pocket limit is reached	Members will pay no more than $2,100 in out-of-pocket expenses in the calendar year
S4	$34,470 individual $46,530 couple***	No	When a member reaches the limit to trigger the "donut hole" at $2,970, Prescription Advantage will begin covering any difference between the individual's co-pay under the Medicare plan and the co-pays listed in the next column	$12 for generic drugs or $30 for brand-name drugs for a 30-day supply once deductible limit has been reached. This co-pay structure will continue until the member's out-of-pocket limit is reached	Members will pay no more than $2,515 in out-of-pocket expenses in the calendar year
S5	$57,450 individual $77,550 couple****	$200 annual premium to be covered	Members pay their drug plan's deductible (if any) until their out-of-pocket costs for covered prescription drugs total $3,355 as a Prescription Advantage member in the calendar year 2013. After that, they will pay $0 for prescription drugs covered by their plan	Members pay full Medicare drug plan co-payments	Members will pay no more than $3,355 in out-of-pocket expenses in the calendar year

* These amounts are 188% FPL
** These amounts are 225% FPL
*** These amounts are 300% FPL
**** These amounts are 500% FPL

this annual out-of-pocket limit is reached, Prescription Advantage will cover drug co-payments for the remainder of the plan year."[42]

Fishing Partnership Health Plan[43]

Responding to the fact that 43 percent of fishermen in Massachusetts were uninsured, 30 percent had delayed seeking medical care because of this, and around 34 percent were below 200 percent FPL, policy entrepreneurs from the Massachusetts Fishing Partnership, a non-profit umbrella organization representing the state's various fishing industries, received support from the commonwealth's legislators to create a non-profit health provider, which launched in 1997. The Fishing Partnership Health Plan (FPHP) provides coverage to anyone who earns over half of their income from fishing, along with their families, and has over 2,000 subscribers—except that it is not currently taking new members and is transitioning individuals to the health insurance marketplace. The FPHP is offered through a local provider (currently Harvard Pilgrim Health Care), and is partially funded through the support of the federal government and the state. Insureds pay 60 percent of the premiums, whatever their incomes are, and FPHP will pay the rest.

There is a widely held myth that any person, business, or other entity that can be insured will actually be able to find insurance, and this is simply not the case. What we see in the example of the Fishing Partnership Health Plan is yet another example of the public–private system that pervades the American approach to the safety net. When the market failed, the government simply could have stepped in with its own program, but instead, it worked to create a system that is administered by the private sector, while backed by assurances of the public one. With the introduction of the Affordable Care Act and its policies in January of 2014, we once again see that public–private cooperative system.

Healthcare for Veterans

The United States federal government and the Commonwealth of Massachusetts offer a variety of healthcare programs for veterans. The largest is TRICARE,[44] the military's healthcare system, and is available to around 9.6 million Americans[45] and draws upon the services of fifty-six military hospitals and 361 health and dental clinics.[46] TRICARE offers a variety of health plans for active and retired military members and their dependants, but for our purposes is not all that relevant since it is not means tested nor does it offer any protections for those who cannot afford the premiums. For those individuals, the United States Department of Veterans Affairs offers services through a program known simply as the VA health system, but note that the system only covers injuries sustained or aggravated in the line of duty. Other treatments may be provided, but they must be paid for either out-of-pocket or through health insurance.

VA Health System

Veterans are eligible for the VA health system if they served twenty-four months in the military and left under any condition other than a dishonorable discharge, unless they were unable to serve that long due to hardship or an injury sustained or aggravated in the line of duty. To apply, a veteran fills out form VA 10–10EZ, which asks all the routine questions about one's date of birth and address, and also asks about financial information and certain other service-related questions, like whether one received a Purple Heart or was exposed to radiation in the line of duty.[47] Once the application and supporting materials have been received, the VA will place the applicant in one of eight categories (see Table 5.12) to help determine who will be admitted and in what order, since there are far more applicants than the facilities can serve.

The costs charged to individuals in the VA health system depend on what Priority Group they are in. Table 5.13 presents the income thresholds for the members of Group 8, with those falling below the income levels receiving free care, although it bears repeating that the only care given is to treat injuries sustained or aggravated in the line of duty. The payment schedules are seen in Table 5.14.

Given the nature of the clientele it serves, the VA health system offers a wide variety of services that may be specific to the needs of individuals who have served in combat. The Veterans Administration tracks, for example, individuals exposed to Agent Orange, those who had been in Hiroshima or Nagasaki after nuclear devices were deployed, and those who had possibly been exposed to depleted uranium. In the 232 community-based Vet Centers found in all fifty states and protectorates individuals can receive a wide range of counseling services to help them transition back to a healthy and productive civilian life, including marital counseling and grappling with post-traumatic stress syndrome. The VA also provides prosthetics for those who have lost a limb, and up to $6,800 to help alter one's home to make it accessible. Blind veterans can receive seeing-eye dogs, and there is also a suicide prevention hotline staffed around the clock at 1-800-273-TALK (8255). Both the VA and the states maintain a wide array of nursing homes and other care facilities. Veterans can stay at a federal veterans' home if they require "nursing home care for life or for an extended period of time for a service-connected disability, and those rated 60 percent service-connected and unemployable; or veterans who have a 70 percent or greater service-connected disability."[48] The VA also maintains 131 cemeteries for veterans in thirty-nine states, where they can be interred at no cost.[49]

States can also maintain veterans' homes. The Texas Veterans Land Board operates eight facilities that provide long-term care. The cost is $148 per day, with eligible veterans getting $95.82 of that paid for by the U.S. Department of Veterans Affairs. The rest must come from out-of-pocket or insurance (including Medicare).[50] These facilities are also

Table 5.12 VA Health System Priority Groups[51]

Group	Characteristics
1	Veterans with service-connected disabilities rated 50% or more and/or veterans determined by VA to be unemployable due to service-connected conditions
2	Veterans with service-connected disabilities rated 30 or 40%
3	Veterans with service-connected disabilities rated 10 and 20%; veterans who are former Prisoners of War (POW) or were awarded a Purple Heart medal; veterans awarded special eligibility for disabilities incurred in treatment or participation in a VA Vocational Rehabilitation program; and veterans whose discharge was for a disability incurred or aggravated in the line of duty
4	Veterans receiving aid and attendance or housebound benefits and/or veterans determined by VA to be catastrophically disabled
5	Veterans receiving VA pension benefits or eligible for Medicaid programs, and non service-connected veterans and non-compensable, 0% service-connected veterans whose gross annual household income and net worth are below the established VA means test thresholds
6	Veterans of World War I; veterans seeking care solely for certain conditions associated with exposure to radiation during atmospheric testing or during the occupation of Hiroshima and Nagasaki; for any illness associated with participation in tests conducted by the Department of Defense (DoD) as part of Project 112/Project SHAD; veterans with 0% service-connected disabilities who are receiving disability compensation benefits and veterans who served in a theater of combat operations after November 11, 1998 as follows: 1. Veterans discharged from active duty on or after January 28, 2003, who were enrolled as of January 28, 2008 and veterans who apply for enrollment after January 28, 2008, for 5 years post discharge 2. Veterans discharged from active duty before January 28, 2003, who apply for enrollment after January 28, 2008, until January 27, 2011
7	Veterans with income and/or net worth above the VA national income threshold and income below the geographic income threshold who agree to pay co-pays*
8	Veterans with income and/or net worth above the VA national income threshold and the geographic income threshold who agree to pay co-pays*

*The VA national income threshold and the geographic threshold for the cities are found in Table 5.13.

Table 5.13 Regional and National Income Limits for Free or Subsidized VA Services for Members of Group 8[52]

Veteran and Number of Dependants	Boston Income Threshold	Houston Income Threshold	Kansas City Threshold	Los Angeles Threshold	New Orleans Threshold	National Threshold
0	$50,050	$41,195	$45,210	$51,975	$38,115	$30,978
1	$57,200	$47,080	$51,645	$59,400	$43,560	$37,175
2	$64,550	$52,965	$58,080	$66,825	$49,005	$39,304
3	$71,500	$58,850	$64,515	$74,195	$54,450	$41,433
4	$77,220	$63,580	$69,685	$80,135	$58,850	$43,562
5	$82,940	$68,310	$74,855	$86,075	$63,195	For each additional dependant add $2,129

Table 5.14 VA Health System Cost Structure for Services[53]

Inpatient Care	Priority Group 7 and certain other veterans are responsible for paying 20% of VA's inpatient co-pay or $236.80 for the first 90 days of inpatient hospital care during any 365-day period. For each additional 90 days, the charge is $118.40. In addition, there is a $2 per diem charge. Priority Group 8 and certain other veterans are responsible for VA's inpatient co-pay of $1,184 for the first 90 days of care during any 365-day period. For each additional 90 days, the charge is $592. In addition, there is a $10 per diem charge
Extended Care	For extended care services, veterans may be subject to a co-pay, based on each veteran's financial situation and is determined upon application for extended care services and will range from $0 to $97 a day
Medication	While many veterans are exempt for medication co-pays, nonservice-connected veterans in Priority Groups 7 and 8 are charged $9 for each 30-day or less supply of medication provided on an outpatient basis for the treatment of a nonservice-connected condition. Veterans enrolled in Priority Groups 2 through 6 are charged $8 for each 30-day or less supply of medication; the maximum co-pay for medications that will be charged in calendar year 2013 is $960 for nonservice-connected medications
Outpatient Care	A three-tiered co-pay system is used for all outpatient services. The co-pay is $15 for a primary care visit and $50 for some specialized care. Certain services are not charged a co-pay
	Co-pays do not apply to publicly announced VA health fairs or outpatient visits solely for preventive screening and/or immunizations, such as immunizations for influenza and pneumococcal, or screening for hypertension, hepatitis C, tobacco, alcohol, hyperlipidemia, breast cancer, cervical cancer, colorectal cancer by fecal occult blood testing, education about the risks and benefits of prostate cancer screening, and weight reduction or smoking cessation counseling (individual and group). Laboratory, flat film radiology, electrocardiograms, and hospice care are also exempt from co-pays

open to surviving spouses and Gold Star parents, defined as those who have lost a child in active duty.[54] The state of California has eight homes for a total capacity of over 3,000 residents.[55] For veterans fifty-five and over, these facilities provide a wide range of outpatient services, have some assisted living quarters, and also maintain long-term beds.[56] California's veterans pay for services at the homes on a scale pegged to their incomes, with a cap, as follows:

- Residential Care: 47.5 percent of income, up to $2,400 per month
- Residential Care for the Elderly or Assisted Living: 55 percent of income, up to $4,500 per month
- Intermediate Care: 65 percent of income, up to $5,000 per month
- Skilled Nursing Home Care: 70 percent of income, up to $5,600 per month.[57]

Texas maintains four state veterans' cemeteries, where interment is free for anyone eligible. Those who died due to service-related causes may also receive up to $2,000 to help cover costs associated with a funeral home.[58] California, in contrast, does not maintain its own veterans' cemeteries (although there are nine national cemeteries located in the state),[59] but will still cover some of the expenses. If the death was service related, the state will contribute up to $2,000 for transportation and burial expenses, otherwise, the amount will be up to $300.[60] It bears noting that in America all indigent individuals can be buried for free, care of their local community, in places known as "Potter's Fields."[61]

Conclusion

As we saw walking through the case of Massachusetts, the health programs offered to the poorest are bewildering. Even though they have a definite logic to them, it is extremely difficult to comprehend, and even then, the math behind the subsidies and tax credits is daunting, and significant percentages of those in need of these programs simply lack either the time or the analytical abilities to become comfortable with these programs. As a result, enormous numbers of adults and especially children who are eligible for free or highly subsidized healthcare do not enroll in programs. Indeed, if nothing else, what this chapter reveals once again is the incredible importance of social workers in the lives of the poor. Social workers are the entrance to virtually all the programs listed in this book, and while it is beyond the scope of the text, one cutting-edge element of the American welfare state concerns the efforts of social workers to ensure that all who are eligible are enrolled in the various programs, since the programs are simply far too complicated for many, if not most, of those eligible to enter into on their own.

That being said, the Affordable Care and the health insurance market-places are making the American social safety net far more comprehensive. American households with incomes of under 400 percent FPL will have access to extremely good health insurance, with subsidized premiums and co-pays. While this insurance may still not be cheap, health insurance in America is expensive, which is a simple reality. But it is now available to all who want it, since no American can be denied coverage during the annual open enrollment periods each fall. 2014 and 2015 are going to be years where somewhere between seven and twenty-one million individuals flood into the insurance system—and as a result, the routine healthcare system as well. These early years of the health insurance marketplaces are going to be very exciting for those following health policy, and the quicker one comes to understand how marketplaces function, the easier it will be to see how the lives of millions of previously uninsured Americans are impacted.

Notes

1 https://www.healthcare.gov/glossary/essential-health-benefits (accessed August 2013).

2 http://kaiserfamilyfoundation.files.wordpress.com/2013/01/8303.pdf (accessed August 2013).

3 The costs of paying for universal coverage all fall in part on employers of over eleven people, who must either offer healthcare plans to their employees with a "fair and reasonable" contribution toward the costs, or help subsidize public insurance options by paying up to $295 a year per employee.

4 The form can be found at http://www.mass.gov/eohhs/docs/masshealth/appforms/mbr.pdf (accessed August 2013).

5 http://www.insurancepartnership.org/index-html.asp (accessed August 2013).

6 http://www.healthcare.gov/using-insurance/low-cost-care/childrens-insurance-program/index.html (accessed August 2013).

7 http://www.insurancepartnership.org/documents/IP_Company_Brochure.pdf (accessed August 2013).

8 https://www.mass-health-insurance.org/masshealth-how-can-i-apply?&usck=1 (accessed August 2013).

9 http://www.massresources.org/masshealth-standard.html or the official site: http://www.mass.gov/eohhs/consumer/insurance/masshealth-coverage-types/under-65-and-families/masshealth-standard.html (accessed August 2013).

10 http://www.insurancepartnership.org/documents/IP_Company_Brochure.pdf (accessed August 2013)

11 http://www.mass.gov/eohhs/consumer/insurance/masshealth-coverage-types/under-65-and-families/masshealth-commonhealth.html (accessed August 2013).

12 http://www.mass.gov/eohhs/consumer/insurance/masshealth-coverage-types/under-65-and-families/masshealth-family-assistance.html (accessed August 2013).

13 http://www.mass.gov/eohhs/consumer/insurance/masshealth-coverage-types/
under-65-and-families/masshealth-basic.html (accessed August 2013).

14 http://www.mass.gov/eohhs/consumer/insurance/masshealth-coverage-types/
under-65-and-families/masshealth-essential.html (accessed August 2013).

15 http://www.mass.gov/eohhs/consumer/insurance/masshealth-coverage-
types/65-plus-at-home/masshealth-limited.html (accessed August 2013).

16 http://www.mass.gov/eohhs/consumer/insurance/masshealth-coverage-types/
under-65-and-families/masshealth-prenatal.html (accessed August 2013).

17 https://www.mahealthconnector.org/portal/site/connector/template.MAX
IMIZE/menuitem.3ef8fb03b7fa1ae4a7ca7738e6468a0c/?javax.portlet.tpst=
2fdfb140904d489c8781176033468a0c_ws_MX&javax.portlet.prp_2fdfb14
0904d489c8781176033468a0c_viewID=content&javax.portlet.prp_2fd
fb140904d489c8781176033468a0c_docName=connector%20outreach&javax.
portlet.prp_2fdfb140904d489c8781176033468a0c_folderPath=/About%20Us/
Other%20Resources/&javax.portlet.begCacheTok=com.vignette.cachetoken&
javax.portlet.endCacheTok=com.vignette.cachetoken (accessed August 2013).

18 https://www.mahealthconnector.org/portal/site/connector/template.
MAXIMIZE/menuitem.3ef8fb03b7fa1ae4a7ca7738e6468a0c/?javax.portlet.
tpst=2fdfb140904d489c8781176033468a0c_ws_MX&javax.portlet.prp_
2fdfb140904d489c8781176033468a0c_viewID=content&javax.portlet.prp_2fd
fb140904d489c8781176033468a0c_docName=Income%20Guidelines&javax.
portlet.prp_2fdfb140904d489c8781176033468a0c_folderPath=/About%20
Us/Connector%20Programs/Eligibility/&javax.portlet.begCacheTok=com.
vignette.cachetoken&javax.portlet.endCacheTok=com.vignette.cachetoken
(accessed August 2013).

19 See two pdf files: "Health Benefits and Co-pays Effective 7-1-13eHHhh" https://
www.mahealthconnector.org/portal/binary/com.epicentric.content
management.servlet.ContentDeliveryServlet/About%2520Us/Common
wealthCare/CommCare13%20Renewal/HealthBenefitsAndCopays.pdf
and "Enrollee Premium Contribution Comparison" https://www.mahealth
connector.org/portal/binary/com.epicentric.contentmanagement.
servlet.ContentDeliveryServlet/About%2520Us/CommonwealthCare/
CommCare13%20Renewal/EnrolleeContributionComparison.pdf (accessed
August 2013).

20 http://www.massresources.org/pages.cfm?contentID=48&pageID=13&
subpages=yes&dynamicID=681 (accessed August 2013).

21 https://www.mahealthconnector.org/portal/site/connector/ind-overview.
Note, the data used a Boston zip code, for someone not qualifying for MassHealth
subsidies, with one adult and two children. Go in and explore!

22 www.mass.gov/eohhs/docs/masshealth/deskguides/fpl-deskguide.pdf (accessed
August 2013).

23 http://www.massresources.org/pages.cfm?contentID=48&pageID=13&
subpages=yes&dynamicID=683 (accessed August 2013).

24 Medically necessary treatments are defined as "necessary: healthcare services that
diagnose or prevent an illness or disability, or that cure conditions that are life-
threatening or cause illness or pain."

25 Which is actually an acronym for "Combined Omnibus Budget Reconciliation Act." See http://www.dol.gov/dol/topic/health-plans/cobra.htm (accessed August 2013).

26 http://www.massresources.org/pages.cfm?contentID=50&pageID=13& subpages=yes&dynamicID=695 (accessed August 2013).

27 http://www.medicareconsumerguide.com/medicare-part-a.html (accessed August 2013).

28 People over sixty-five and those who are younger but disabled can buy in to Part A by paying $461 per month in premiums. Those who have contributed thirty to thirty-nine months in Social Security would pay $254 per month in 2010.

29 www.medicare.gov/Pubs/pdf/11579.pdf (accessed August 2013).

30 http://www.cms.gov/Regulations-and-Guidance/Guidance/Transmittals/ downloads/R72GI.pdf (accessed August 2013).

31 http://www.cms.gov/Regulations-and-Guidance/Guidance/Transmittals/ downloads/R72GI.pdf (accessed August 2013).

32 www.medicare.gov/Pubs/pdf/11579.pdf (accessed August 2013).

33 The Health Care Reform Act of 2010 will eliminate the extra subsidies over time.

34 www.medicare.gov/Pubs/pdf/11579.pdf (accessed August 2013).

35 http://www.medicare.gov/MPDPF/Public/Include/DataSection/Questions/ SearchOptions.asp (accessed August 2013).

36 http://www.medicare.gov/part-d/costs/coverage-gap/part-d-coverage-gap. html (accessed August 2013).

37 For the federal government's Medicare website, go to http://www.medicare.gov/ part-d/. Unfortunately, the website is poorly designed. A far more useful website for the researcher is operated by the Kaiser Family Foundation: http://kff.org/ medicare/ (accessed August 2013).

38 http://www.ssa.gov/pubs/10525.html#a0=0 (accessed August 2013).

39 http://www.mass.gov/elders/healthcare/prescription-advantage/prescription- advantage-overview.html (accessed August 2013).

40 http://www.mymedicarematters.org/PrescriptionDrugs/ExtraHelp/do_i_ qualify.php (accessed August 2013).

41 http://www.massresources.org/prescription-advantage-medicare.html (accessed August 2013).

42 http://www.mass.gov/elders/healthcare/prescription-advantage/ (accessed August 2013).

43 http://fishingpartnership.org/ (accessed August 2013).

44 http://www.tricare.mil/ (accessed August 2013).

45 http://www.tricare.mil/Welcome/MediaCenter/Facts/BeneNumbers.aspx (accessed August 2013).

46 http://www.tricare.mil/Welcome/MediaCenter/Facts/Facilities.aspx (accessed August 2013).

47 https://www.1010ez.med.va.gov/sec/vha/1010ez/Form/1010EZ-fillable.pdf (accessed August 2013).

48 http://www1.va.gov/opa/publications/benefits_book/benefits_chap01.asp (accessed August 2013).

49 http://www.cem.va.gov/bbene_burial.asp (accessed August 2013).

50 http://www.glo.texas.gov/vlb/veterans-benefits/veterans-homes/what-will-I-pay. html (accessed August 2013).

51 http://www1.va.gov/opa/publications/benefits_book/benefits_chap01.asp (accessed August 2013).

52 For regional thresholds, see http //www.va.gov/healthbenefits/resources/gmt/ index.asp. For national thresholds, see http://www.va.gov/healthbenefits/cost/ incomethresholds_2012.asp (accessed August 2013).

53 http://www1.va.gov/opa/publications/benefits_book/benefits_chap01.asp (accessed August 2013).

54 http://www.glo.texas.gov/vlb/veterans-benefits/veterans-homes/eligibility. html (accessed August 2013).

55 http://www.calvet.ca.gov/VetHomes/LevelsOfCare.aspx (accessed August 2013).

56 http://www.calvet.ca.gov/VetHomes/FAQs.aspx#vhc3 (accessed August 2013).

57 http://www.calvet.ca.gov/VetHomes/FAQs.aspx#vhc3 (accessed August 2013).

58 Eligible individuals are as follows: veterans and members of the armed forces, certain members of the military reserves and Reserve Officer Training Corps, commissioned officers of the National Oceanic and Atmospheric Administration and Public Health Services, World War II Merchant Marines, Philippine Armed Forces, spouses and dependants (if under twenty-one and unmarried or twenty-three and under if still in school. (http://www.glo.texas.gov/vlb/veterans-benefits/ veterans-cemeteries/eligibility.html) (accessed August 2013).

59 http://www.cem.va.gov/cems/state.asp?State=CA (accessed August 2013).

60 https://www.google.com/url?q=http://calvet.ca.gov/Files/VetServices/ Module9G.pdf&sa=U&ei=PDu-UIjMKI6tiQe3z4GwAg&ved=0CAcQFjAA&c lient=internal-uds-cse&usg=AFQjCNH_4kqDk5XqebehEPtVgCNeiOmMkA (accessed August 2013).

61 In Boston, the "Potter's Field" is located in the Fairview Cemetery in the Hyde Park region of the city. Houston has two. The old one is on Oates Rd (which has over 13,000 individuals interred there), while a new one is on Crosby Eastgate Rd (http://www.houstonarchitecture.com/haif/topic/23755-harris-countys-new-potters-field-in-crosby/). Kansas City managed to lose track of the potter's field that served it from 1911 to 1965, known as Leeds 1 and Leeds 2 (divided by Interstate 435), which holds an estimated 10,000 or so individuals (http://www. columbiatribune.com/news/history-buried-in-potter-s-fields/article_1cfd4a68-7702-5a8c-b8d6-c8a4f6bf8261.html). The current potter's field is on 1600 N 94th St. In Los Angeles, the dead are cremated and interred at Evergreen Cemetery. New Orleans' field is in Holt Cemetery (accessed August 2013).

Chapter 6

Conclusion

The challenge in describing the American welfare state is that it varies from place to place. Thus, we selected five cities that vary, not just geographically but also in both the levels of benefits and the types of support provided. The social safety net is always on the forefront of policy innovation, and this is so for two reasons. Firstly, the need for assistance constantly outreaches the ability to supply it, and thus policymakers are constantly scrambling to be more efficient and effective. This is true for affordable housing in many if not most cities, and is true for virtually every other element from meeting nutritional needs to obtaining healthcare to getting enough income assistance to keep one's household afloat. Moreover, the political and socioeconomic contexts in which public policies are delivered change over time. The massive public housing projects built in the mid-twentieth century came to be seen as too large to be healthy for those who resided there or nearby, leading to smaller developments and voucher systems. Post-Katrina New Orleans, while admittedly an extreme outlier, once again provided an opportunity to reflect upon what kind of housing to provide for the city's poorest. But this is true in every policy area, in every part of the country. We are seeing a wide range of inventive policies to ensure children eat a healthy breakfast every day, for example, and in recent years have witnessed states exploring public–private partnerships in matching training for those on TANF and Unemployment Insurance with the needs of the given state's employment needs. Even with the age-old concern for meeting the income needs of the nation's poorest, the larger context in which they are embedded shifts with the economy. TANF was born in the mid-1990s under a long economic upswing, and that was a very different context from our current situation where the nation is working to recover from the largest recession since the 1930s. Moreover, this first element—that of underlying need and of policies to confront it—is deeply embedded in a second element; that of how different members of the American polity understand the nature of poverty and need.

Policies are created to deal with perceived problems, but how those problems are perceived is highly political and contested, and this is just as true for the proposed solutions to solve them. The great challenge to confronting poverty in

America through the creation of a social safety net is that Americans cannot even agree that many aspects are even problems, let alone whether they can be rectified, or even whether they should be. This, of course, is where this book comes in, since if we want to discuss anti-poverty programs, we should at the very least know what the current ones are.

The programs described have been presented largely without comment in order to allow researchers of all political leanings to turn to this short book as the foundation for approaching a variety of questions. At the policy level, this work arms the reader to ask which policies are coherent and logical. Is it clear what the perceived problem is, and does the policy address it adequately? Are the policies seamless, or do they leave gaps? What are their target populations, and if some are left out, who are they, and does it make sense to exclude them given the problem being addressed? Can we think of approaches that would be more effective, or more efficient? Would programs meet their goals better if private contractors provided the services rather than government employees, or the other way around for those currently privately provided? We can also examine how the same individuals or households—in the argot, the "target populations"—are addressed in different policy areas. Are they treated more generously in some areas than others, and from a policy perspective, do these differences make sense? Readers may want to compare income limits for various programs (including such things as funds allowed to be put aside for burial expenses) and ask why they differ, sometimes dramatically.

This book also provides grist for the mill at the political level. Put simply, what do we perceive as problems when we think about the nation's neediest, and how should the American polity seek to deal with them? Each of the four policy areas described above deal with their own specific concerns, but now we come to see that they are also connected to one another in interesting ways, allowing us to think about them at an abstract level as well, asking larger questions about the goals for them. Do we want policies to lift people out of poverty? To encourage the poor to get out of poverty, but not lift them out through assistance? To lift certain elements of the population out of poverty—be they veterans, the elderly, or children, for example—but not others, such as able-bodied adults? On what grounds would we justify that? How should those residing in this country illegally be treated? Likewise, should some be denied assistance if they have criminal records, and if so, for how long?

These are big questions, and they speak very directly to the nation's identity. In general, we have learned two key points from studying public policy. First, people are more likely to support those who seem similar to them, and when one enters the literature on the welfare state, one immediately confronts the question of "us" and the "other." We saw this in the brief history that started this book, with white policymakers designing Social Security retirement benefits in a manner that exempted large swathes of the black population. Is it possible that even today, many Americans are ambivalent about TANF because they see recipients being different from themselves?

Second, policymakers tend to divide the needy into the categories of the "deserving" and "undeserving" poor. Nowhere does the idea of the "deserving" come across so clearly as when we compare how adults are treated versus children, and the reason, I suggest, is because children are universally seen as being powerless to shape their own situations. It is a rare twist in American politics where those who are politically the weakest are the ones who receive the most help. We have seen this over and over, with children obtaining benefits that their parents or guardians do not. While veterans and the elderly vote in disproportionately high percentages and reap attention because of it, children rely on others to advocate for them, and those voices, frankly, are rather weak. Children are supported by the American political system because policymakers understand that they cannot fend for themselves. How else can we make sense of the fact there are health programs where the family's income is so low that the children qualify and yet the parents still do not?

So we end this book with questions. The policies we have read about affect the lives of the recipients in stunningly profound ways. Hopefully, now that you have a deeper understanding of the many programs discussed, you are better armed to think about both what you consider the problems the United States faces in confronting poverty, and what you want the solutions to look like.

Index